Larry Skeats was born in 1936 in West Ilsley in Berkshire, moving to Breamore in Hampshire when still a boy. After completing his National Service in the Royal Hampshire Regiment, in 1956 he moved to Wimborne St Giles, Dorset, following in his father's footsteps as a shepherd. From 1963 he was the shepherd on the Crichel Estate, looking after a flock of over 2000 sheep.

Just before Christmas 1987 he hung up his crook for the last time, beginning a new career as a publican. Since 1993 Larry and his wife Sue have owned The Trooper Inn, Stourton Caundle, in the heart of the Blackmore Vale, turning it into one of Dorset's most popular pubs, famous for its collection of rural bygones. Larry is well-known for his talks on shepherding.

A SHEPHERD'S DELIGHT

LARRY SKEATS

THE DOVECOTE PRESS

First published in 2001 by The Dovecote Press Ltd
Stanbridge, Wimborne, Dorset BH21 4JD

ISBN 1 874336 94 6

Designed and produced by The Dovecote Press Ltd
Printed and bound by the Baskerville Press, Salisbury

A CIP catalogue record of this book is
available from the British Library

1 3 5 7 9 8 6 4 2

Contents

I

A Country Childhood

I was born in 1936 at West Ilsley in Berkshire, horse-racing country, where Dick Hern, who trained the Queen's horses, had his stables. My parents lived at a farmstead called Starvall, off the beaten track, way out from the village. I remember moving down into the village to a cottage in Well Lane. Our furniture was moved with a horse and four-wheeled wagon. My Mother and I walked the one-mile distance, with my sister in the pram.

My Father was second shepherd to Ike Wakefield on the Lockinge Estate, owned by Captain Lloyd. Ike was one of the finest shepherds ever born, and came out of the same mould as one of Dorset's well-known shepherds, John Randal. What those two didn't know about sheep wasn't worth knowing. The times I've heard Father say, 'If only old Ike were here now'.

The most distinctive thing I remember about Ike was his big, white moustache. He nearly always wore a brown smock-coat, buttoned up the front, a necktie and brown gaiters. Both Father and Ike had Old English Sheep Dogs. Collies weren't heard of then except in Scotland. A speedy dog wasn't necessary with hurdle flocks such as Hampshire and Dorset Downs. I've seen those dogs sit by an open hurdle, while carrying the forward hurdles through for the following day, to save keep opening and shutting it, and the ewes wouldn't attempt to go through it. The same applied when they filled the hay cribs. The dogs would hold the sheep back until told to do otherwise.

One dog of Father's was called Moses. He lived in an old wooden cider barrel for a kennel. Nailed at the top was an old West of England sack, which would be pulled down over the entrance if it was cold or windy. At first we would do it last thing at night, but after a while, we would only have to go to the back door, and he would tug at it with his teeth, and settle down. Cider barrels make good kennels because the bulge in the barrel makes a natural-shaped bed, with an old rug in it. Another trick that old dog used to do was, if you said 'die', he would roll over on his back, with his legs in the air, and lie motionless. Well, sometimes he would wag his tail, but if you said 'die' again, he would be completely 'dead'. I don't know why, but that breed of dog seldom barked, so Father put a small round bell on his collar, so the ewes would be aware of his presence.

I spent many a morning with Father, slowly walking the flock across a field of winter wheat. It was far better than rolling it. Their little hooves firmed the ground and they nibbled the wheat, which was good, because it made it send out more shoots. Sometimes, if a crop was strong and weather conditions right, the shepherd would even fold the sheep over the whole field, with the hurdles. The first time I saw that done, when the ewes had finished, you couldn't see a blade of corn left, and I thought, 'That's finished that off'. But about a week later it started to grow, and you've never seen a field of wheat like it. It was cut with the horse-drawn binder and was used to thatch the Estate houses. That's why sheep are referred to as the 'golden hoof' on the land. It's like rolling and manuring all at the same time. Some of the old-fashioned farmers even do it today, but not very often.

About six weeks before the ewes were due to start

lambing, they were fed once a day. The cake was put into galvanised troughs, and the ewes were let back behind to feed. Then, after three or four days, you had to move the troughs on, to keep up across the field. Most of them had two wheels at one end, so Father would pick up two and roll them on. I used to help, holding the trough with both hands and walking backwards. One day, not realising or remembering where the big water troughs were, I reversed into one. The tank hit me behind the knees, and I fell straight back into it. It was nearly full of water and I was like a drowned rat. They were too busy to take me home, so I had to sit in the shepherds' hut with a coat round me, while my clothes dried around the old tortoise stove.

The cart-horses always brought the water to the sheep folds. Like the cake troughs, the larger water troughs had four wheels and a ring to be pulled by. It was usually the trace 'hoss' which pulled them. That was the horse at the front, if there were two. They would bring three or four water barrels a day. There was no water laid on in those days. Sometimes, when the carter came past our house to go up to the sheep, I would have a ride on top of the water barrel.

If they were hauling mangolds, I would ride up and back again. If the sheep were in a field with a bit of a slope and they had several cart-loads to do, instead of taking the trace horse all the way back to the clamp, I would stay and hold him at the bottom of the field, ready to hitch him back up to pull the heavy load up across to where Father wanted the mangolds chucked out.

One day, when the carter was taking water up to the sheep, the horse in the shaves shut his wind and dropped dead. I remember watching it happen from about five hundred yards away. Father ran across to see if he could help. He let the water out of the back and helped the carter hitch off the trace horse. It was the first time I had ever seen a dead Shire horse. It brought tears to my eyes, more so because it was one of my favourites. He was called 'Sargent', a beautiful creature, almost black, with a lovely shiny coat. I had ridden him bare-back dozens of times, round and round in the village pond in the winter time to clean his feet of mud before going into the stable, after a day's ploughing or dung hauling.

Once I was given the job of walking one horse round in the pond for about a quarter of an hour, with a four-wheel wagon, just to tighten the bonds on the wheels, where they had come loose through not being used for a while. It's great fun when you're only nine or ten years old. Not all the kids in the village were allowed to do it, just two or three of us, whose fathers worked on the farms, and they knew we could do it sensibly.

Summer was always the best – at harvest time, leading the horses from stook to stook, loading the wagons, taking them to the yard where the rick-builders were, and bringing the empty ones back out. We were allowed to ride on the carts going out, with the long reins. Sometimes we would get sixpence a day given to us, but we didn't do it for the money. It was good fun to us, and we liked helping out. On one occasion I was taking a slightly younger mare out into the field and one of the laders fell forward and frightened her. She bolted, with me on the cart with the long reins. She ran all the way round the cornfield. I managed to steer her round, missing everything and not letting her through the gates. Eventually she ran out of steam and calmed down. I led her back to where we were supposed to go and started loading again – and, strange as it may seem, I wasn't frightened.

I can remember my first day at school in West Ilsley. We were allowed to play with toy trains all morning, and with coloured chalks on small blackboards in the afternoon. I realised later on that this was a ploy to introduce us to school and make us like it. Funnily enough, I loved my school days. I think it was because I was always told to do as you were told and to try your best. I've tried to do this all my life, and I don't think I've done too badly.

I can recall the old steamroller man, with his green caravan on the back of the roller, moving into the village. He stopped next to the pond, where he could get his water for the engine. He stayed for about three weeks, living in the van. My mother would cook him one hot meal a day. His name was Mr Spracknell, and I often think of him when I see Fred Dibnah on TV. He was very much like him. When he drove past our house, I would put a ball-bearing on a penny, and the steam roller would nearly push it right through the penny. Because Mother cooked him a hot meal, I was allowed to have rides on the steamroller.

Mr Spracknell also had a huge, round tar boiler, with a fire box underneath. The pitch, or tar, came in forty gallon metal barrels. There was a swinging chain lift on the side of the boiler, which lifted the barrels to empty them into it. The Council would deliver about half a ton of coal for the tar boiler and his tortoise stove in the hut.

We boys would go to the local baker's shop and buy a loaf for tuppence. Then we would sit with Mr Spracknell and have toast with him. We didn't eat much butter in those days. We would have beef dripping. Mother made little dishes of it for us to take up and have on our toast, and a bigger one for Mr Spracknell. It wasn't always beef as we used to eat a lot of mutton in those days as well. Mother also made her own lard, from pigs Father kept down the garden. Butter was for her only, except on Sundays. Then we children had it with bread and jam. Cake was also only for Sunday's tea. Mother made it on Saturday and it always took pride of place on a cake stand in the middle of the family table. Our mouths would dribble looking at it, but we were made to eat at least two slices of bread first. We couldn't just have cake. If we were really lucky we had jelly.

I was the eldest of six children, and still am. I had to help Father in the garden, and my next two oldest sisters, Margaret and Jean, had to do the washing up every night. I remember how they would moan if it was raining and Father and I couldn't get on in the garden. 'We've had to wash up,' they'd say, 'and he ain't done nothing'.

One night I said, 'I'll do the washing up. You two go out in the garden and help Father'. They thought they were onto a good thing. What they hadn't realised was that they had to work for an hour. Washing up only took about ten minutes. That particular night, Father dug up all the old Brussels sprout stumps, about eighty, and Margaret and Jean had to carry them and put them in the chicken run. They never complained after that.

I had four sisters and a brother, in that order, and when Mother and Father were alive, we were a very close family. Unfortunately, they both died in their late fifties, and since then we have drifted apart, as some families do. It is a great shame. My Gran outlived my Father and, because we had moved from West Ilsley to Dorset by then, I didn't like the idea of her up there on her own, as my Father was an only child. Reluctantly, she moved to Dorset and, for four years, she lived for about two months at a time with me and two months with my eldest sister, Margaret. She was a dear old lady. Some days I would tease her for fun, and she would say, 'If only I could get you across my knee, I would tan your bottom, my lad'.

She was born in 1888, in Ilsley, two doors away from where she lived most of her life. She had a pine kitchen table, which we would all sit around as children. I don't think the top of it ever saw daylight. It was as white as a lily. She always had three layers of these old plastic-coated tablecloths on it, which you could wipe off after meals. On Sundays there was always a lovely white lace cloth. She used to say, 'Those were my grandmother's tablecloths when I was a little girl'. When she cleared the table she would pick up the cloth by all four corners, go to the door and shake the crumbs out for the birds. All mums did that until the modern way of life started, with formica or place mats on a plain table. Even starch has almost disappeared now.

Gran would never throw away any old clothes or material. She used to make fireside rugs with it, on a hessian sack. She'd cut it all up into pieces, about three inches by one inch, and, with a special hooked needle, pull it through the sack and back up through. Then, when it was finished she would line the back. I remember the rugs as being snug and cosy, but, alas, very dusty. If you didn't shake them out every day, it was like a cloud of smoke. They were also used as bedside rugs, and were great favourites with cats, if you had one, and most families did.

Gran also had a chaise-longue which had never seen the light of day. It was always completely covered up. In the bay window there was a huge three-seater Victorian rounded-arm settee, which was also covered up. When we went to visit her with Mother and Father on a Sunday, Father would point to a certain seat, and that was where you sat until he told you different. He was a very strict disciplinarian. When I was about six years old, he gave me one good hiding with his big, wide belt, and I have never forgotten it to this day. He would never tell you to do anything twice – though he could be obstinate himself. If he had to do something or go somewhere that he didn't want to, he'd say, 'I'd sooner have my ass rubbed with a brick.'

It's not like that today. I was in the company of a certain family not so long ago and I counted the parents tell their boy nine times to get undressed ready for bed. The ninth time I said, 'Do you realise that's the ninth time you've told him that, and he still defies you and sits there?' Then they got angry with him and pulled him off the settee. He started undressing, pulled his jumper off, threw it on the floor and then moved on a little further. Off came his shirt, straight onto the floor, then his vest, trousers, pants and socks, until he reached the bathroom. There were all his clothes in little heaps. I can't begin to imagine what my parents would have said or done. His mother walked behind him, picking it all up. I just couldn't stop myself from passing my opinion, and I said, 'I would have made him come back stark naked in front of us all and pick it all up'. This was a boy of ten.

When I was ten I was given my own small garden patch, and whatever Father planted, I would plant too. When his friend or my uncles came along and said, 'Well done, lad', I felt 'as proud as a louse' and ten feet tall, even more so when Father helped himself to something from my plot to enhance his own exhibit at the local flower show. At one show, Father was being presented with a cup and one of his mates shouted out, 'Good job his o' boy is a good gardener'. He received the cup, stepped back and gave it to me to hold – and I was hooked for the rest of my life.

At Harvest Festival Father always gave vegetables to decorate the church. He wasn't one for going to church himself, but I was made to go every Sunday morning and evening. I joined the choir at eight years old and loved it. There were ten of us boys, all dressed in a red cassock and white surplice. Then there were ten or twelve men behind us in black and white. In those days, nearly half the village would be there. I eventually got the job that no one else really wanted. That was to light the altar candles just before the service was about to begin, and then have to put them out when they sang the second hymn, the second line of the second verse. I never really knew why it had to be so precise. It was the vicar's choice, and he would always be looking at me, and he would nod his head as if to say, 'Go'.

There was also Sunday School in the afternoon. We all had a stamp book, and at each attendance, we would be given a religious stamp to put in it. On Plough Sunday, if the weather was fine, the choir and the whole congregation would walk about half a mile up to the village allotments to hold the service. The vicar would lead the way, then the choir, then each family group. On one of those occasions, I was privileged to follow the vicar, carrying the cross.

During this time we had moved from Well Lane Cottage to number 7, which was a three-bedroomed house. We had an evacuee who came to live with us there, in about 1941-2, and I will never forget his name, and neither would you. It was Victor Sylvester. I often wonder if he is still alive. He was the same age as me, and he stayed with us for four years. He was a dirty little sod, and he used to wet the bed from time to time. I think it was partly due to the circumstances he had been through in the London Blitz. He had been in the thick of it. He wouldn't go to bed unless a candle was left burning all night. He was absolutely terrified of the dark.

Because of Victor, I can understand why all these Londoners who move into the country want street lighting.

But we don't want them. That was when most of the courting took place, in the darker evenings – or so I've been told! If you look on some stone bridges or stiles, and even in the bark of trees, you can see the evidence in the form of hearts and carved initials. Every man and boy carried a pocket knife, and usually a piece of string and a penny. Then it was said that you could, 'cut, tie and buy'. Another thing a lot of men had in their pocket was a lucky stone. Whether it worked or not, I'm not sure, but I always had one, and I've been a fairly lucky man. There's not a lot I would wish to change if I had a second chance.

I've enjoyed my life, and think how lucky my generation has been to live through such extraordinary times. We've seen the motor car develop, the carthorse disappear, the first tractors appear on farms, and the last binders almost vanish. Some are still used for cutting thatching straw. We've seen the hand-milking of cows become a thing of the past. Sheep shearing by hand shears has gone, and you had to work hard then to do three score and ten a day. We have passenger aircraft, and who of us, fifty years ago, ever imagined Concorde and rockets to the moon. Animal rights and anti-hunting campaigners – where were they then, when the first dog was sent to the moon?

Some things have been almost reversed, like using an outdoors toilet and always eating indoors. These days the toilet's indoors and we eat outdoors on barbecues. But the best advances have been in medical research and hospitals. I've got a super G.P., Dr. Geoff Sparrow at Stalbridge. He is always concerned about my welfare and health, in that order, because his first question is, 'What real ales have you got on now, Larry?'

Let's go back to West Ilsley, 'when I were a boy'.

My best friends were Gordon Dew, John Verney and

Derek Allsop. I have seen all three in the past few years, but we did have long periods, and I mean forty years, not meeting up. Derek came and found me out last year. He's been a successful businessman in the building trade, and he lives in Newbury. Gordon and I used to live next door to each other and were once inseparable. His father was farm foreman on the same farm as where my Father was a shepherd. Just below our house was the sheep dip, and we would always help at dipping time, moving the sheep around, opening gates and such like. We would start with them at six in the morning, and would hope they hadn't noticed the time, so we could maybe miss school, but at half past eight, Father would say, 'You'd better get indoors and get ready for school'.

Gordon and I had a four-wheel cart we could sit on together and ride down the hill into the village. We steered it with our feet and a piece of string. We would do this sometimes to get to school, leave it at a friend's place, and take it back at night. It was made out of pram wheels, the two at the back slightly bigger than those at the front. Our feet were the brakes. Most kids had them in those days, but I haven't seen one for years. Today it's skateboards and scooters, custom made, and costing hundreds of pounds. School dinners then were two shillings a week and each of us had a third of a pint of milk free every day.

We didn't have a sports' field, just a closed-in tarmac playground with goal posts painted on the wall. The ball we used was about half the size of a normal ball. You can imagine the arguments about whether it was in or had hit the post, but we were always told to respect the referee's (teacher's) decision.

I believe it was in about 1945 or 46 when Father was given new Lister electric shearing machines. They had three of them hanging from the beam in the old tythe barn. Something somewhere wasn't quite right, and they all got an electric shock from the machine. It nearly knocked them over and it took the hand-piece out of their hands. It was to do with the earthing. Electricity hadn't been in the village long. Not all houses were on it either. My Granny Skeats had it put into her old cottage eventually, but because of the incident in the barn, she wouldn't use it. She was scared stiff to put it on. She'd had it about two weeks and still used the old oil lamps. I remember going up to see her one evening. She was filling the lamp with oil, so I said, 'Look, Gran, this is all you have to do,' and I put the switch down. 'How do I put it off?' she said, so I showed her that several times, and eventually, she had enough courage to use it. Even after that she still used the lamp, to use up the oil she had left. I told her she should have kept it, in case of power cuts. The next day she went out and got another gallon as a standby. She was afraid to use the electric 'because the bulb would get hot and burst'.

One thing Gran Skeats always had plenty of was coal. She must have had nearly two tons in her old wood shed, but she knew someone was taking some of it from time to time. She suspected her neighbour, so we put a lock on the door. One day Gran had to nip to the shop, so I stayed at her cottage till she got back. The neighbours hadn't realised I was there, saw her go out and thought the coast was clear. But I was watching, and saw this neighbour go into Gran's shed. I rushed out, slammed the door and put the bolt across. I locked her in there until Gran came back, and, as luck would have it, the village policeman was peddling by. They didn't pinch any more after that. He'd made a note of it in his book.

That family was, though, thank God, in the minority.

There wasn't a lot of thieving in those days. Half the time, people never locked their houses, and if they did, the key was always under the doormat. Churches were never locked either. You could always go in and look around. What happened to all that trust?

Father always had a bob or two in his pocket. Sometimes he would lend a few shillings to the local jockey lads, and they would always pay him back on Friday, pay day. But one of the lads avoided Father for a couple of weeks, owing money. One night he went into the Harrow pub and Father said, 'Where's my money that you owe me?' He said he hadn't got any and asked if he could leave it another week. Father knew they'd had a winner in the week, and would have won some, so he bent down, picked up this little jockey by his ankles, put his feet on the ceiling and shook the money out of his pockets. It frightened the others to death. They never borrowed from Father again.

About three weeks after that incident, about eight of them came up to our house in the evening. They knocked on the door and said they had come up to give Father a good hiding. 'Just a minute,' he said, 'I'll put my boots on and I'll be out'. I had heard this from my bedroom window, and looked out, bearing in mind that Father was a big man. He weighed about fifteen stone and feared no one. He laid out five or six of them and the others ran away. The next morning I went out in the road where this had taken place, and picked up two or three pounds. There were coins everywhere.

Because the jockey lads were black and blue when they turned up for work next morning, the boss wanted an explanation. He made all eight of them go back the next evening and apologise to Father. They respected him after that, and were always giving him tips from the stables. One by the name of little Tommy McGuire used to come to lunch on Sundays. Father's cousin, Tommy Barlow, used to drive the horse box and sometimes Father would go with him.

I went to Newbury with them once, but I didn't enjoy it. Those thin horses, as I called them, pranced about and kicked out too much for my liking. Give me the big, fat Shire horses. I loved them. The heavy cobs were nice too. Father used one of those to pick the rams up from nearby farms, if he bought one or maybe two. I would go with him for the ride, in the old rubber-tyred float. We would trot there and walk back.

2

In Father's Footsteps

Sadly, in 1948, a recession hit sheep farming and Father was made redundant. He had to look for another shepherd's job. Sir Westrow Hulse at Breamore had a small flock of Hampshires, but didn't show them. His was one of the oldest established Hampshire Down flocks in the country, and he invited Father to look around. He asked Father if he would like the job and start showing again. That was a real challenge to him, so my family moved to Breamore in Hampshire.

Although Breamore was only about sixty odd miles south from West Ilsley, it was another country to me. I had to learn to call a gate a 'wicket'. Stakes, which held the hurdles up, were 'shores', and the string loops that secured the hurdles and shores were 'shackles' not apses. 'Come here, son' became 'Yer, lad'.

The change I remember most was the number of apple trees. Every garden had at least two, and there were little orchards here and there. In Ilsley you could count them on one hand. The first year there I'd never seen so many apples before, and, sure enough, there were several cider makers in Breamore, including Bill Roberts, Stan Ponting and Bill Dymott. Mr Dymott used to give Father a bottle or two, and when my uncles came to visit, he would uncork a bottle. They thought it was marvellous, until they got up to go outside. I can still see them now, falling about and singing.

One of them came back in the autumn to help with the

cider making, he was so intrigued with it. Of course, he drank quite a lot of the fresh juice as it was being pressed. He was supposed to go back home on the service bus on Sunday night, but he couldn't leave the toilet long enough for another forty-eight hours. He learnt very quickly not to try the cider for at least a year, and, better still, two years, if it was kept properly. Bill tried to cool him from drinking too much of it by telling him that he put a dead rat in it to feed off, but it didn't put him off. He came to stay with us for a few days every year, just to have a drop.

In 1948 I was at Breamore Church of England School. There were three classes, Infants, Juniors and Seniors. The School had gardens which were divided up, so that each boy had a little plot. Each plot was about six by ten feet. Each week the boys were given a mark out of ten. When the vegetables reached their peak, places were awarded – first, second, third and so on. Terry Mouland and myself were close buddies and our plots were next to each other.

I had seen my father plant some kale, which germinates quickly, so Terry and I got hold of some from the farm buildings at Home Farm on the Breamore Estate. We took it to school and, for a prank, we threw it onto all the other gardens, not thinking that our own plots would be the only two without any on when it came up. It came up like a plague!

You can guess the rest. Our garden tutor was Mr. Jack Gilbert and he made Terry and me go out and hoe and hand weed all the other boys' gardens. We didn't really mind as it meant missing other lessons, and we loved gardening anyway. The best part was that, about six weeks later, we won the first and second prizes. Terry won the first prize. After all, his father was a good gardener on the Breamore Hulse Estate. He worked in the walled-in gardens, which are now the Breamore Countryside Museum. At least a third of it was covered with greenhouses and glass frames.

Terry, his brother Derek and I were among the privileged few who were allowed into what seemed to be the sacred walled garden. We helped the gardeners to open the cold frames, some six inches, others a foot and some all the way off. Then we would go round in the evening and close them up. What I liked most was being allowed to turn the wheel which opened and closed the greenhouse shutters in the roof. The other bonus was seeing all the wonderful fruit trees that were there, especially the peaches and pears. It was in that garden that I saw my first real peach.

On Saturdays in the winter Terry and I were made to saw up enough logs to last a week. We used to do mine first with a small bow saw. Then we went to Terry's place and his Father would allow us to use his big cross-cut saw. We felt so proud to be allowed that privilege, and it gave us the chance to saw up more and bigger logs. In those days, the men always seemed to have an abundance of wood stored in their gardens. I think it was a perk that went with the job, along with free milk, a load of manure and some dredge corn for the chickens. We always had fifteen to twenty hens running around free range to keep us in eggs. The cottage also went with the job. My parents never paid any rent. It was known as a 'tied' cottage.

I was probably one of the few boys who enjoyed school. I always had top attendance figures. I was Head Sports captain for the football team. We played other schools such as Godshill, Fordingbridge, Downton Hale and Redlynch. We had quite a good team – Cyril Parker, Geoff Herridge, Terry and Derek Mouland, Dennis Young, Micky Vincent, David Vincent, Brian Slade, Ivan Webb, Doug Harding, John Coffin, Eric Hillman and Jim Beck, to name but a few.

Sports day was always Friday afternoons, on the Marsh. I always remember marking out the school football pitch. We didn't do it with whitening or creosote. We bigger boys put out a long string line, the full length of the pitch, then, with a spade, neatly cut down into the turf about four inches deep and three inches wide, turn it completely upside down and roll it absolutely flat. It used to last the whole season – penalty areas as well.

Before a match we had to take a wheelbarrow and spade to clear away cow pats because farmers had the right to graze their cows on the Marsh. In the evenings and at weekends I worked for one of the farmers, Mr Ernie Ponting. I hand-milked the cows, so when the final whistle was blown on Friday afternoons, I would ask our Head Teacher, Mr Fuller, if I could be excused from 'fall out' to start gathering the cows from the Marsh. I only had to start calling for the cows to recognise my voice and start moving towards the farm, which wasn't far from the pitch.

Mr Ponting had about twelve or fourteen cows, which I would tie up with the old cow chains. I'd give them a handful of hay and start hand-milking. Sometimes I'd milk half of them before Mr Ponting appeared. Even his wife used to help with the milking. Many a time, if they were hay-making, I milked them all on my own.

I was twelve or thirteen years old then. On Saturdays I did a paper round from Breamore Station. I started at seven in the morning and finished at half past eight. Then I went straight to Mr Ponting's to help him to deliver milk round the village. We had two tradesman's bikes. We finished that at about half past ten and then I was treated to breakfast with them. After that I went to get his heavy horse in from the field, brush him down and harness him up. I had to stand on an egg box to reach his head collar and bridle. The saddle was heavy, but I always seemed to manage somehow. Then I hitched him into the two or four-wheel carts and went off to get mangolds, cow cabbages, straw or sometimes hay to last the rest of the week.

Mr Ponting also used to grow his own potatoes, plough them in with the horse and single-furrow plough. I planted the potatoes up the side of the furrow while he ploughed. He planted every other two furrows, so I didn't have much time to waste. The field was about two hundred yards long, and he'd have about thirty-five or forty rows. The next job was hand-hoeing two or three times, but he earthed them up with the horse drawn bulker, and I had to lead the horse. While walking with the horse, about every two or three yards I had to drop a marrow seed, which obviously got buried. I had to do this about every sixth row. Later on, each Tuesday we would send the marrows to Salisbury and Ringwood markets or sell them at the gate. We used to load a 'dung-putt' full at a time and bring them back to the farm.

He grew mangolds too. We drilled them in with the horse and horse-hoed them when they first came up. Then I had to hand-hoe them and single them out. When they were ready to harvest we pulled them individually by hand, cut the leaves off, put them into small heaps and sometimes covered them with the leaves. In a day or so we would pick them up with the horse and cart and make a clamp close to the farm for use in the winter. We had to make sure they were protected from the frost, so to do that we covered them with a thick layer of straw, which we then covered with fairly dry, rotted manure. We had to keep the sides steep to let the rain run off, so that it wouldn't soak into the clamp.

Mr Ponting used to make quite a lot of hay. He would cut the water meadows between Breamore and Charford; the large ones with the horse-drawn mower, the small ones and the corners with an Allen scythe, and the really awkward bits with a hand scythe. There was never anything wasted or not cut. We even raked it up by hand with a wooden rake. It was really hard work hand pitching it onto his two- or four-wheeled horse-drawn wagons. He would take one into the farm, which was about one and a half miles away. The part I liked most was taking the horse back on my own to pick up the second cart, while Mr and Mrs Ponting unloaded the first. While they unloaded the second I started milking the cows. By this time, Mr Ponting had bought a new cow and she had about three tries at kicking me out of the cowshed. I always left her till last, hoping he would come and milk her. She was such a devil, he eventually sent her on to Ringwood market, where she was bought and used as a nurse cow.

During all this time I was paid a shilling an hour. I remember having to tell Mr Ponting that I wouldn't be able to work on Saturdays any more as I'd been invited by Mr George Biddlecombe to go as a beater on the Breamore Estate and would be getting seven and sixpence for that day. After three or four weeks, Mr Ponting said he would pay me the same to work for him until one o'clock every Saturday. I never wanted to work Saturday afternoons because we used to go to football. Breamore had two teams then. Eventually I was asked to play for the reserves, and later for the first team, alongside players like Percy Marlow, Norman Biddlecombe, Eddles Young, Cyril Bailey, Bill Marlow, Bill Northway, Stan Waterman, Doug Harding, Mike Piercey, John Noble, Geoff Herridge and my old pal, Terry Mouland.

Sometimes. on the way home from school, Mr Tanner, the blacksmith, stopped me and asked if I would turn the handle of his sandstone sharpening wheel. He usually asked two of us, so that we could take turns as it was quite hard work. He would have axes, billhooks, reap hooks, garden shears and all sorts of things, even wedges from the timber cutters. What makes me smile now was how Mr Tanner would watch out for my sister, who came out of school a quarter of an hour earlier than me, being in the Juniors. He would say to her, 'Tell your mother Laurie will be a bit later today. I need him.' He took it for granted that we would do it and he gave us sixpence.

I can still remember having to do it on my own one day. I seemed to go into a trance, just standing there winding away. Once he left to talk to someone in his forge and he shouted back, 'You can stop now, lad'. I thought he was still there sharpening. The old wheel squeaked and he wouldn't oil it as he could tell if we were going too slow or too fast. After a while he progressed to a treadle wheel, which made me redundant. The wheel had water in the bottom instead of a tin at the top with a brass tap dripping away. As soon as he had given us our sixpences, we used to walk back to Mr Candy's shop and spend half of it on sweets. We kept the other half for the next day.

I can honestly say that I never ever had pocket money given to me by my parents. I always earned it. I've always had a £1 in my pocket, and I've always said I would never be rich and never broke. And sixty years on, that's still my philosophy.

It was the same with clothes. My mother never had to buy any for me after the age of thirteen. I always saved and bought my own.

There was another Mr Ponting, Stan, at Upper Street in the village of Breamore. He was a cousin to the Mr Ponting I worked for. One day he said to my father, 'Do you think that o' boy of yours would come and do some work for me?' So, one Saturday morning I went down to see him and, to my delight, he wanted me to chain-harrow and roll three of his grass fields at the back of his farmhouse with his Shire horse. I was over the moon at being able to drive this beautiful animal and walk behind the chain-harrow and roller with the long reins. To be in control of that horse with the power that it had was a boy's dream come true.

From then on I wanted to be a carter, but my father had other ideas. He said, 'It's no good taking that up. There won't be a hoss left in two or three years' time.' And how right he was! Within the next two years, both Mr Pontings had small tractors, like grey Fergusons and a Fordson Major. The last of Stan Ponting's Shire horses gave cart-horse rides on the Marsh on Coronation day. I have a picture of my sister in fancy dress on that last horse.

Talking of dress, Mr Stan Ponting nearly always wore a red handkerchief round his neck, a black bowler hat, braces and plus fours with black leather gaiters. He was always smartly dressed, especially when going to Market.

It was in about 1949-50 that my father started to think about my future, knowing that I would soon be leaving school. My father was Head Shepherd on the Breamore Estate, working for Sir Westrow Hulse, and he was adamant that I should follow in his footsteps and those of my grandfather and be a shepherd. It seems that he was right and I worked as a shepherd for the next forty odd years. I had helped my father from time to time from the age of seven. I used to stand in gaps in the hedges, gateways etc. when moving the flocks at lambing time. I fed orphan lambs and stood for what seemed like hours when a ewe was giving birth, to make sure the lamb didn't get smothered in the afterbirth or drown in the water. He used to say, 'As soon as it's born, move the lamb to the front of the ewe, just far enough in front of her so she'll have to get up to clean it'.

When the ewe had become attached to her lamb, or if she had twins, I would put them in an individual coop, where they would stay for about forty-eight hours. This was repeated probably twenty or thirty time a day, when I'd be up there Saturdays and Sundays, sometimes in snow storms, or on cold, rainy days. Wet days were the worst. Sheep don't mind dry, cold weather, but they don't like it when it's very wet.

Father had all sorts of ways of predicting the weather, according to the mannerisms and movements of the sheep, and he was seldom, if ever, wrong. If it was going to rain, the ewes would prance and jump when running: if it was about to snow, they would go to the highest ground in the field, not necessarily the most sheltered part.

Because of having to go to school, I was only allowed to sit up at night with Father on Fridays. I used to love it – living in the shepherd hut, with the old tortoise stove for warmth, a cup of tea and sacks of sheep cake to sleep on. I felt so grown-up doing things like that. I felt like a full-grown man, or at least I acted like one. In fact, all through my life it seems as though I have been at least three years ahead of my age. I always wanted to be doing things with my father or other adults.

By the time I was eleven or twelve I could carry hurdles and pitch a fold. I started by carrying one hurdle, then two and eventually, four. I remember Father marking out the forward fold and sticking a stake in where the line of hurdles was to be pitched. He would pitch one side and either Mr Bill Waterman or I would pitch the other. It was seldom we would be any more than a foot out when we met. That was probably twenty-five hurdles square, a distance of fifty yards. Most Saturday and Sunday mornings I had to take the whole flock down into Breamore Park and let the ewes graze the soft, lush grass, and it also kept the parkland around the Big House tidy.

I had two dogs to control the ewes and it was most important not to let them roam into Breamore House gardens and onto the lawns, or to let them escape out of the two main drive entrances. It was also awkward when the keepers had the pheasant rearing pens in the park, up close to the woods. The sheep weren't allowed near them either.

I remember one day Sir Westrow's dog, a chow, strayed into the park. He spooked the sheep and they ran towards the pheasant pens and tipped two of them over, releasing the chicks and the old mother hen. Norman Biddlecombe, the keeper, was furious, but he did see what happened, luckily for me. As we were trying to stop the chow from chasing the ewes, Norman said, 'If I had a gun, I'd shoot him.' Well, as it happened, I had a catapult and several pebbles in my pocket, so he said, 'Go on, then. Let him have one of them!' And from about thirty yards, I hit him, smack on the rump. He soon made off for the House, and we never ever saw him again in the park at rearing time.

Norman obviously told his father, George, about the incident and how good I seemed to be with the catapult, so the next time he saw me, he put me to the test with it. He put his penknife in the top of a gate post and said, 'Let's see how really good you are.' And, believe it or not, I hit the handle clean off, leaving the blade still stuck in the post. I don't know whether he was surprised or disappointed, but his words were, 'Don't you ever let me catch you shooting at my pheasants!'

In those days you didn't do that sort of thing because, if

anyone was caught poaching or shooting a pheasant, it was instant dismissal, and you were homeless. As Father was Head Shepherd, on shooting days he was usually given one anyway. In his job he also had the privilege of wiring and ferreting rabbits on the Estate. He had an agreement with the keepers, Bob, George and Norman Biddlecombe, as to where he could place the snares. They were always between home and wherever the sheep happened to be, so that the keepers knew whose wires they were.

I will now let you into a fifty-year-old secret. I think it's a shame to take it to the grave, as I believe I'm the only one alive who witnessed it. The other two, my father, and the under-shepherd, Bill Waterman, are both long gone.

On our route to the sheep, up Upper Street Lane, we had to pass several houses, the last being that of Mr Bill Dymott. He was Head Carpenter on the Estate and he had a lovely big cat, which belonged to his late daughter, Dorothy. This cat had, over two days, partly eaten some of Father's rabbits, which were caught in the wires. At this stage, Father and Bill Waterman were unaware that it was a cat which had done it. They thought it might be a fox or a stoat. So they left one of these rabbits where it was, made a circle with twigs etc. and set a gin trap in the entrance to where the rabbit was. Lo and behold! The next morning, on their way to work, they saw this lovely big cat crouching there, firmly caught in the trap, still alive, but with two broken legs. Knowing the history of the cat and how much the family thought of it, we knew there would be a hue and cry about it. We decided the best thing to do was to put it out of its misery, so Bill gave it one almighty blow on the head and killed it. Now they had the big problem of where to bury it, knowing full well that the Dymott family would search high and low for their pet.

We took the cat to the lambing pen and did all the necessary work as usual before lunch at ten o'clock. Then, while having their namet (bread and cheese), they decided that the best and safest place would be under the steps of our shepherds' hut, where the ground was always well trodden. I had to dig the hole and make sure it was at least two feet deep, which I did.

For over a week friends and the family searched everywhere within a mile of the house – rabbit holes, fox earths were dug up, as we knew they would be, but, of course, to no avail. Mr Dymott came to father twice and said, 'Shep, did you kill our Dorothy's cat?' And my father, quite rightly, said, 'No'.

They had one more last search for the cat and were then going to give up. Bill Dymott came down to the lambing pens where we were sitting having our dinner. He stood on the bottom of the steps of the shepherds' hut and said, 'Shep, I'm going to ask you one more time. Did you kill our cat?' And still Father said, 'No', because it was his mate who had actually killed it. Little did Bill Dymott know that he was within two feet of the cat, standing on top of its grave!

I believe Norman and Edna Dymott are still alive, and, if so, I hope they will forgive Father and Bill after all these years. At least, they will die knowing what happened to Dorothy's cat.

That was some lambing season. Father was struck down with sciatica and could hardly move. I always thought it was an act of God to punish him for what they had done with that cat. It then came down to me. Although still a young lad, I took Father's turn at sitting up at night in the shepherds' hut, miles from nowhere, and did the lambing for him. This was for about a week in January, on alternate

My parents, Albert (Bert) and Doris, on their engagement day at
West Ilsley, Berkshire, 1934.

Below left: My mother and I on my Christening Day, 1936.

Below right: My grandmother, Catherine Skeats, with
Father's Old English Bearded Collie 'Ben'.

Me, Father and Bill Waterman in 1953: the Breamore Estate shepherds.

Below left: Shearing with a Lister petrol engine in Breamore Park in 1953 when I was seventeen, just prior to going into the army to do my National Service.

Below right: Outside my home in Breamore in 1955 on leave from the army.

Passing Out into the Royal Hampshire Regiment at Lower Barracks,
Winchester, in 1954 after my ten week initial training.

The Lord Shaftesbury's XI that played against the Black and White Minstrels
Showbiz XI at Wimborne St Giles. The present Lord Shaftesbury is seated in
the centre. Their captain, and goalie, was Leslie Crowther.
I am in the top row, one in from the right.

Crichel House, near Witchampton, the home of Commander and the Hon. Mrs Toby Marten, where I was the shepherd for more than twenty years.

Bringing the flock from Crichel Down to Cock Road Farm for lambing in 1970.

One of the three shepherds' huts on the Crichel Estate. They were used for shelter in extreme weather, and for storing spare clothes, medicines, and sacks of food for the ewes and their lambs. A shepherd's hut is part of my life, and I haven't been without one for over half a century.

Keeping a watchful eye on the heavy in-lamb ewes on Crichel Down in 1978. These days, only a handful of farms still use wattle hurdles as lambing pens.

The 1920s shepherd's hut I used to live in during lambing on the downs. My Border Collie 'Ben' was named after Father's.

My three children, Belinda, Sandra and Roland, at Cock Road Cottages,
Crichel Estate, in 1965.

Belinda and Sandra as 'tom-boy' teenagers in the 1970s on Crichel Down. They
could work with dogs, sort pens, and could have had flocks of their own.

Me with twin orphaned lambs brought back in from the field.

nights with Bill Waterman.

Colonel Jimmy Stanford, the estate agent, found out that I had so called 'bravely' done this for Father and that I was leaving school at Easter. He asked me if I would like a job on the Estate, so I said 'yes' straight away. They increased the flock numbers and I was third shepherd, in those days known as the 'Teg' shepherd. That meant looking after the young ewe lambs, kept for replacements. My first week's pay, for seven days, was forty-nine shillings – or seven shillings for an eight hour day – less than a shilling an hour. I gave Mother £2 and kept nine shillings for myself.

The young ewe lambs were always folded with wooden hurdles and kept two or three fields away from the main flock. I had about sixty of these to pitch out for every day. Sometimes they were on grass and red clover, sometimes turnips or hungry-gap kale. The hardest thing to pitch hurdles and carry them through was oats and vetches. Sometimes the vetches were three feet high, the same as the hurdles. Many was the time I fell over with the hurdles and shores on top of me, and sometimes when I let the ewes into a new fold the vetch was so tall you couldn't see them.

One frightening incident I shall never forget happened on a Saturday morning, out in Breamore Park in 'higher ground'. I had to pitch out for Sunday's fold and there was a tremendous thunderstorm overhead. Normally I would have gone up to the shepherds' hut out of the rain, lightning was flashing everywhere. However, we had a football match in the afternoon, so I just had to get the work done before dinnertime.

Well, to make a hole for the shores to go in, I had an iron pitching bar. I had just finished making the hole, hit the bar into the ground ready for the next hole and let go of the bar, which was only an arm's length away, when the lightning struck the bar. It was like a firework in reverse, running down the bar into the ground. I can assure you that I didn't pick up the bar and finish the fold off until the next day. It was a very nasty experience.

I can recall another experience with lightning striking. It was twenty-five years later on the Crichel Estate. I had three ewes and four lambs killed, by the side of an electricity pole. What I have never been able to work out is why the lightning tore part of the fleece off the ewes, so that it ended up stretched in a long line along the ground, about ten yards away. We couldn't claim on the insurance as it was classed as an 'act of God'.

With the pedigree flock of Hampshire Downs we had at Breamore, we used to go to all the shows, including the Royal Show. Over the years my father won every prize it was possible to win, and could claim to be the first shepherd to sell a ram for over £1,000. If I remember correctly, it was to Mr Stewart Tory of the famous Shapwick flock, who went on to sell sheep all over the world.

Other great memories I have of Breamore were the annual flower shows and fêtes in the lovely park. There was a tug of war with teams from Poole Police and Upton Oil Company, in which six out of the eight were all brothers by the name of Cuff. Bill Cuff, the captain, was a great character. My father won 'bowling for a live pig' several times. I can still see him now, bringing the pig home in a 'West of England' sack in a wheelbarrow. From then on, it was my job to feed it twice a day, and I cried whenever he had the pigs killed. They were killed in the garden and burnt with straw to get the hair off them. Then they were pulled up into the apple tree to be gutted etc. We were always given the bladder to make into a football because, as you know, the only thing not used or eaten from a pig is his squeak.

I won first prize at the village show once, for catching the most white cabbage butterflies, about three or four hundred, I believe it was. I used to catch them by swiping them with a pea stick, and putting them in a tobacco tin. Then I took them down to Mary Stanford on the Marsh in Breamore and she recorded the catch twice a week.

Another memory of the show was the adults' and children's fancy dress. It was nearly always Jack Gilbert who won the adults' competition. One particular year he made a full-size grandfather clock, in which he could stand up and just about shuffle along. At the end of the show, he gave it to me, and I had it in my bedroom for years. It had a wooden frame with cardboard and was painted dark brown. It very much resembled Big Ben.

In the vegetable classes, Father always did well. Usually the best overall collection of vegetables included good onions and shallots. He used to grow his parsnips down pipes to get the length. We never had a flower in the garden. He said, 'Flowers are no good. You can't eat them.'

I have good memories too of the annual Harvest Supper. It was held in the Breamore House 'Long Room', and was for all the staff - from the farm, the keepers, the gardeners, chauffeurs – all the employees. Breamore House seemed very special to me. It's a beautiful Elizabethan house. We used to graze the sheep all around it, in the park itself and also in the field known as Front Park. I always wondered what was in such a large house.

To be allowed into the Long Room each year for the Harvest Supper was more of a privilege than the meal itself. The food was always local – venison from the woods, lamb and beef from the farm and vegetables from the walled-in garden. It was the one time of the year when all the employees were together under one roof and were all treated as equals. Sir Westrow and Lady Hulse greeted us all on arrival. Their son, Master Edward mingled with the staff. It really was a special evening. I revisit at least once a year to see Master Edward, and also the Countryside Museum there. It means a lot to me. It's a must for everyone to see. John Forshaw, the Curator, is an old friend of mine. He's always a pleasure to talk to and is very welcoming.

3
Finding my Feet

It was about now that I was due to do my National Service. Father tried to stop me going because I could have got a two-year deferment. There were three or four lads going in at the same time, and I said to him, 'In two years' time they'll be coming out, and at twenty I'll be going in. No way! I'm going.' And I did. I joined the Royal Hampshire regiment in Winchester for two of the best years of my life. It certainly taught me discipline. There is very little discipline today.

I did my ten weeks' training, which was hard, but good. Believe it or not, because I was a shepherd boy and could shear sheep, I was sent to Aldershot for three weeks on a barbers' course. Then I was sent back to Winchester barracks and was there for the duration of my time. This was lucky for me because I always enjoyed sports. I played football for the Regiment, and hockey. I also boxed for the Regiment. My greatest night, I remember, was boxing at the Connault Drill Hall in Pompey, and getting a drawn decision against a chap from the Paras' Regiment. I used to spar with Kenny Lawrence from Bournemouth. He was a southern area champion. I played football with Ray Crawford, who played for Pompey, Ipswich and finally, for England. I also had the privilege of shooting at Bisley for the Regiment, in the 'all ranks' team.

Besides cutting hair some days, I was a regular Fire Point Instructor on the ranges, training new recruits as they came in. I remember that one recruit kept firing up above the bullseye. I told him that to correct that he would have to shoot at six o'clock, which meant lower down. He said that he couldn't do that because it would be too dark. He said, 'I can hardly see the target now and it's only half past four.

When we had a new intake arrive, they were marched round to my barber's shop, ten at a time, for their first haircut. One particular lad was a 'Teddy Boy', who said, 'Don't take too much off, mate'. I told him he would have to be the same as the others. He said he wasn't going to, so I just took a little off. I knew he would be back. It was about ten minutes later. He said, 'You've got to take a bit more off'. So I did, knowing that it still wouldn't be enough. Off he went. About ten minutes later again, I could hear someone coming up the passage at the double and one of the training sergeants shouting, 'Left, right, left, right.' I knew exactly who it was. I was busy cutting another chap's hair. The sergeant told this chap to get out of the barber's chair, sat this other bloke down, took the electric clippers from me by force, started at the base of his neck and came out at his crown. Then he said to me, 'Level that up.' It was far higher than it would have been if he had let me do it in the first place. He sat there and cried like a baby. When he came into the army, he thought he was a Southampton 'hard nut', but he had his heart broken in about three days, not only by the sergeants and corporals, but by the other country boys. In ten weeks he was a totally different chap and went to join the First Battalion in Malaya.

I remember vividly the two Christmases I had in the army. A sergeant friend of mine said, 'If you don't mind being away from home, volunteer for the rear party and stay at the camp.' They virtually closed the barracks down, except for the main gate, and the rear party all lived in the sergeants' mess. About twenty of us, officers, N.C.O.s,

everyone – and no rank was pulled. It was great – more
food and drink than we would have had at home. Then we
were home for New Year on double leave.

'Home' was now Dorset; for it was whilst doing my
National Service that my parents moved to Wimborne St
Giles, near Wimborne on the River Allen, where Father had
become Head Shepherd to the Earl of Shaftesbury on the
Shaftesbury Estate.

The time I enjoyed most in the army was playing football
for the Battalion. I used to play for the army on Saturday
mornings, get on my motorbike, go like hell and play for
the village team at Wimborne St. Giles in the afternoon.
Then, after a few pints with some mates, we'd go dancing.
Football today, I'm sorry to say, is not the same. All the
sport has gone out of it.

Wimborne St. Giles had quite a good team, with people
like Ron Flippance, Laurence Blake, Sammy Read,
Malcolm Davis, Colin Chandler, Cliff Blake, Ron Coles,
John Laws, Jack Adlem and Derek Trowbridge; Sid Clarke
was our goalie. Now there was a goalkeeper who needed no
protection from the ref. It was the other way round in those
days. Sid was tall, hard and feared no one. I remember one
Saturday when he went to punch a ball clear and flattened
one of the opposing team, knocked him out for several
minutes. There were no such things as yellow and red cards.
The ref. gave a penalty, and Sid saved it. He said quietly, to
one or two of their players, 'Tell him not to be so close next
time.' When the next corner was given, there wasn't a
player between Sid and the penalty spot.

A really memorable match at St. Giles was against a team
of the Black and White Minstrels. Lord Shaftesbury (then
Lord Ashley) was our captain and the Minstrels' captain
and goalie was Leslie Crowther. It was a charity game, and

I can remember Leslie playing the entire game wearing a large Mexican hat. The match attracted the largest crowd I had ever seen in St. Giles Park. We were given a penalty and the whole eleven Minstrels stood in the goal. Leslie said they were all standing behind the line, so they weren't breaking any rules and weren't interfering with play. The match was drawn 3 – 3 and a considerable amount of money was raised.

In May of 1956 I had completed my two years' National Service. I will admit to almost signing on as a regular at the last minute. It was a good life and there was plenty of scope for promotion, but I knew my parents wouldn't agree to it, especially at that stage of my life. Besides, I had a good home and in those days you didn't go against your parents' wishes. So I got demobbed at Winchester and signed on for five years as a stand-by for the Territorial Army Reserves at Dorchester Barracks. But I was never called back.

It was the start of the shearing season, and I hadn't got a job to go into straight away. At this stage I hadn't met Mr John Ironmonger, the Estate manager, so I did the job I knew best – sheep shearing, with the Harris brothers, Mark and Ted, from Farnham in Dorset.

My first day was at Mr White's in the village of Martin, near Fordingbridge. He had a flock of three hundred Hampshire Downs. Ted, Mark and I all worked off the same old petrol stationary engine, a Petter 5 H.P. twin Flywheel, which, in fact, would drive four units if we wanted it to. I would go as far as to say that those Harris brothers were the tidiest shearers I have ever seen. They were definitely not the fastest, but quality meant more to them, as it did to the farmer who had to look after the flock the other three hundred and sixty-four days of the year.

Another day we were shearing Mr Coward's flock at

Chase Farm, Sixpenny Handley. Being a little younger, and possibly fitter, having just been demobbed, I had a newer handpiece than them. I was shearing nearly two to their one, and they thought it was due to their handpieces running a little hot. They even slowed the engine down, and kept shouting to Trev Carter and Johnny Goodfellow. 'Oil!' And they kept squirting oil onto their clippers. This went on all day – 'Oil! Oil!' I think I sheared about forty more than they did, and to this day, whenever I see o' Trev Carter, he shouts, 'Oil, Larry!' – and that was forty years ago.

Poor o' Johnny Goodfellow has passed on, but I can remember having some wonderful evenings with the Goodfellow family over at the Horseshoes at Ebbesbourne Wake, a lovely little pub, then run by Tom and Gladys. It's still run today by Tom's son, Tony. And if you ever go into the Horseshoes, you'll see that it very much resembles the Trooper at Stourton Caundle. That's because I've tried to emulate it, with all the old 'bygones' hanging around, and adorning the beams and walls. I am luckier than Tony. I have a larger car park where I can also display the old machinery etc. Some of you may have seen it on TV in 1999, when we appeared in 'Country Ways', or on 'Collectors' Lot' on Channel Four.

At the end of the shearing season and with harvest about to start, I applied for a job at Manor Farm at Monkton St. Giles, part of the Shaftesbury Estate. I drove a tractor, corn hauling into the dryer off the combines.

The harvest was good, with heavy yields, and the dryer couldn't keep up, so another tractor driver, Bernard Dunsford, and I offered to work on through the night, burning the midnight oil until about two o'clock in the morning. This went on for about three weeks. We would take two loads of three tons of barley in two cwt. hessian sacks, on an old green Bedford lorry which the Estate had, up to Nine Yews, two miles away. At half-past one in the morning, we double stacked them, so that the floor space in the dryer would be free the next day for Don Parks, the regular dryer man. Sometimes we would do this with wheat, which was in two and a quarter cwt. sacks. Because we worked so late, we didn't get into work the next morning until nine o'clock, instead of the normal seven o'clock. Some of the others thought that Bernard and I were crazy to work these hours, but the money was good on pay day at the end of the fortnight, especially for Bernard, who had six kids. I was saving for a car, and eventually I got one.

My first car was a red and black Morris 8, 1940'ish. Immediately I got it, I put in for my test in Salisbury. I was soon given a date, mainly because I offered to take it on a Tuesday, which most people tried to avoid, because it was market day. It was the easiest thing I have ever done. There was so much traffic in town, I just followed it. I passed the first time, and I shall never forget that afternoon.

On arriving back at St. Giles, I met our own local policeman, P.C. Jeff Weston, on his bike, doing his rounds, a typical good old-fashioned policeman. He used to have a drink with the lads at the Bull, in the village. As I pulled up to say 'hello', and slowly came to a stop, he put his foot on the car running-board and said, 'Well, where have you been, all dressed up?' I said, 'To Salisbury, and passed my test.' I shall never forget the expression on his face. 'You little bugger,' he said. He had always assumed that I had a licence because I had a motorcycle combination and used to drive the estate lorry (but only at night).

The next time he met Father in the pub, he said, 'Your o' boy, the little sod. I always thought he had a car licence.' But I swear he only had admiration for the guts I had in those days and for being sensible, and he said to Father, 'For his cheek, he can drive me and the wife to Bournemouth shopping next weekend'.

In those days, the old village 'bobby' was the salt of the earth. He used to know who was who, and if there was any trouble, which was rarely, he would know pretty well who it was, and nine times out of ten, would give him a severe warning. If he was stupid enough to do it again, he would have him in his little black book. I swear that if we still had the village 'bobby' about, there wouldn't be half the trouble there is today.

After the harvest there were hundreds of straw bales to haul in. We would do this on a bonus/piece-work system. I believe it was £8 per hundred. There were two dairymen, two Estate carpenters, two keepers, Father and myself. Father and I used to finish a bit early so we could go straight to the field and load up two or three large trailers, each holding about a hundred and twenty bales. That gave us a good start and when the others arrived, they could start unloading and stacking in the Dutch barn. Our aim was a thousand to fifteen hundred a night, which was hard work hand pitching, but we could earn almost double the amount we would have done on overtime rate.

The end of September was now upon us and I was taken on officially as shepherd-stockman. The flock was increased from three hundred and fifty to eight hundred the first year, and eventually up to a thousand in the next two years.

The stockman's job was looking after the beef stock, which was housed at Nine Yews, in the old racing-stables which had just closed down and which had been run by Mr Payne-Gallway for many years. The job also meant cutting frosty marrow-stem kale by hand and carting it out to the dairy at Manor Farm. The dairy total was a hundred milkers, Red Polls, and about thirty or forty followers. That would take Sam Selby and me up to about lunchtime. Then I would join Father with the sheep until about four o'clock in the afternoon. After that, it was back to feed the dairy hay and straw, and eventually silage, after the kale had gone.

The Head Dairyman was Carl, a German ex-Prisoner of War, who was a good, hard worker, but who was always whingeing about something. On his day off, the relief milker was my old mate, Bernard Dunsford, who worked long hours with me in the dryer. So, on the evening feeding prior to Bernard's milking the next morning, Sam and I would increase the amounts, and also the morning's feed, and it was surprising how the yield would go up, perhaps five to ten gallons over the hundred cows. Of course, every Tuesday this would be reflected on the daily yield chart on the wall in the dairy. We used to point this out to Carl and say that Bernard was obviously a better milker than he was. He asked Bernard what he did differently from himself, and Bernard said, 'Well, I sing to them all the time I'm milking.' So Carl tried this, but in German, and, of course, it never had any effect. We told him they only understood English, so he would sing in broken English. And Sam and I would increase the kale, hay or silage and he was convinced that it worked. He left soon after that and I often wonder how many people he told that story to.

As the lambing time was approaching, I spent more and more time with Father and the sheep, building the outside lambing pens and doing all the necessary pre-lambing injections etc. We had to trim the odd one's feet if they had foot rot and crutch them all, so they had good, clean back ends. There's nothing worse than handling a dirty sheep if there's a breach presentation where the lambs are born backwards.

Father and I would do alternate evenings and nights. The sheep were never left during lambing. Sometimes you'll hear shepherds and farmers say that sheep never lamb between midnight and five o'clock in the morning, but that's a load of nonsense. When the lamb is ready, he'll arrive whatever the time. As far as the lamb is concerned, it's permanently dark until that little head comes through, and he certainly doesn't know what time it is. I always put their excuses down to a little bit of laziness and the fact that they usually only had small flocks.

The only thing that sometimes slows lambing down a little, be it day or night, is a sudden change in the weather and temperature, especially if there is a cold, wet rainstorm. When that happened we would remark, 'That will make 'em keep their tails down.' But it was only for about two hours, if you were lucky.

Another thing Father would say was, 'Second-rate shepherds always exaggerate the most'. As I grew up I realised it was true, and still is. They are worse than fishermen. Sometimes you'd hear them say, 'I never lost a single lamb.' I'd reply, 'No, but I'll bet you lost some twins and triplets.' There isn't a shepherd born yet who could say that he's never lost a lamb at lambing time.

If you had a good, prolific flock, you had to be there to twin the triplets onto singles. It was always best and more successful to smother the older lamb in the water of the new-born. As long as the two lambs smelt the same, there was a good chance the ewe would take them. You have to introduce the other lamb to the ewe first. After three or four minutes, when the ewe is attached to it, you give her her own. Another tip is always to tie the adopted lamb's feet together, so it can't get up straight away, because, make no bones about it, the ewe will know that a lamb wouldn't be able to stand so quickly, especially if it goes straight to the udder.

Another way of doing the same sort of thing, if you're just too late and there's no water or afterbirth about, is to squirt milk from the ewe over both lambs to make them smell the same. I've seen my father piddle over them, and I've done the same, if there was neither water nor milk and you were under a hedge somewhere, miles from anywhere. Nine times out of ten it worked.

The most expensive and outrageous thing I ever did, using the same method, was when my boss had given me a bottle of whisky to have up in the shepherds' hut 'to keep the cold out'. On the way up to the pen, with the bottle in my pocket, sure enough, there was a big, single lamb and a triplet twenty yards away, just born. I had no water and the ewe had very little milk, so the only alternative was the bottle of Johnnie Walker. I poured as little as possible into the palm of my hand and rubbed it all over the two lambs, and then a drop more to rub round the ewe's nose and mouth. Hey presto! The adoption was complete.

I told the boss the next day, and suggested that perhaps I ought to have another couple of bottles in case it happened again. He laughed and walked away, but the next day, he came up to the lambing pen. I saw him go into the hut and then he came over and asked if everything was OK. With a little smirk, he said, 'I've put another bottle in your hut, just in case.' It was a miniature bottle of Bells.

In those days it was that sort of camaraderie that kept you going. Once a week, the boss would bring a box of groceries for you – soups, tea and sugar, butter and cheese.

One Saturday night, when I was home on leave from the

army, I remember going up to the pens with Father, and there, under the loose straw rick, was an old tramp, sitting there, half-covered with a West of England sack, and, would you believe it, smoking! Father asked him to pack up and be on his way, but he said he was there for the night, and refused to budge. I can still see Father now, picking him up by the scruff of his neck and telling him, in no uncertain terms, to take to the road and never return again.

Two days later we heard he'd done the same thing again at Mr Tozer's lambing pen at Woodcutts near Sixpenny Handley. The police then took him into Salisbury, where there were no barns or straw ricks. which he could easily have burnt down. In the Forties and Fifties there were always tramps around. They had a secret code mark that each one would leave by a gate or on a house where they had been given food and drink, or sometimes money. As children we knew this, but could never work out what the sign was, and still haven't.

It was around this time that electric fencing came along. The first time we used it with the flock there was one ewe which would keep getting out. She would jump over the two strands. So Father thought, 'I'll teach her a lesson and make her respect it.' He caught her with his dog and crook and, being a little naive, he rubbed her nose against the wire. At the time he was wearing heavy, hob-nailed leather boots, and he quickly learnt a lesson – that the current goes to the strongest earth. It went straight through the ewe. She never felt a thing, but it nearly knocked Father over. After this incident, he had a kind of party-trick that he would play on the other old fellows. He would wear his wellies, catch hold of the fence and then ask them to hold his hand. Of course, the same thing would happen to them.

Shearing time came round and Father, Ron Doe and I set

to work. It took about four days to do our sheep, and then we would go and do Mr Way's across at the next farm. He only had about a hundred and fifty, so one day was enough. Eventually we had a gang who came in to shear the flock. They would do the lot in one day. Billy Kinghorn, the gang boss, would shear over two hundred and fifty, and the other three not far behind. His gang consisted of a New Zealander, an Aussie and his brother, Jerry Kinghorn. The hard work then was pulling out the ewes for them from the small pens. I remember the landlord of the Bull Inn, Pete, offering to help. He was a big, sturdy chap and he volunteered to pull out for Billy, the boss, who said, 'Right, if you're up to it, we'll go for the record.' Pete said, 'Right ho!' knowing full well we would all finish up down at his pub. Billy did his first three hundred. I have never seen a man so knackered as Pete was in his pub later. He never had the strength to pull a pint. His wife did the entire session on her own. Pete never offered his services again. We still laugh about it now when Pete comes to play skittles here at the Trooper. He says, 'That was the hardest day's work I've ever done in my life.'

On November 30th, 1959, after a year's courtship, I married a Fordingbridge lass, Georgina Coombs. I'd met her while turkey-plucking the previous Christmas, at the Poultry Packing Station in Fordingbridge. By this time I was full-time second shepherd with Father and I had a cottage, which went with my job on the Estate. My first daughter, Belinda, was born in August 1960. I was helping with the harvest when I got news that Georgina had gone into labour. I got home just in time and was there at the birth to help the nurse. It was a wonderful experience, which I will never forget.

With a wife and daughter, I wanted more money and

more responsibility, but most of all I wanted to be Head Shepherd and have my own flock, so I applied for a job at Aston Tirrold, near Didcot in Berkshire. And I got it, much to my mother-in-law's disgust, because the house with the job was nearly a mile off the road up on the downs. Appropriately enough, it was called 'Sheephouse'. I loved it. It was pure tranquillity. Apart from the sheep, all you ever saw were two strings of racehorses every morning, training on the gallops. They were owned by Mr Cundell. I expect racing people can remember his champion horse, Crudwell. I believe he still holds some sort of record today for the number of races he won.

It was a Mathew Cundell I worked for (a cousin). We'd agreed a wage, but we hadn't mentioned a lambing bonus, which most shepherds had for the extra hours and also as an incentive. We had been lambing a week, and I'd sat up three or four nights when I brought it up. He said that he wasn't going to pay me any extra. It was all part of my job, so I said, 'Well, I won't be staying up at nights then.'

He was one of those farmers who were under the impression that ewes didn't lamb after twelve o'clock, so I asked him if he would meet me at the pen the next day at seven o'clock in the morning, which he did. There were three dead lambs, one ewe with six or seven lambs, two young ewes with nothing, and another with a lamb with only its head out, nearly as big as a rugby ball. So I said, 'Well, what do you think of that lot?'

He said, 'Well, it's up to you to sort it out.'

'Yes,' I replied, 'I can do that, but it takes a while. But what about a bonus?'

A bonus was then about a shilling a lamb. He said, 'No. I have no intention of paying you a bonus.'

I picked up my crook and his two-grain pitchfork, which

I threw like a spear into the ground between his feet, told him to stick the lot up his backside and walked out there and then. Half-past seven in the morning that was. I went home, told the wife, and picked up *The Newbury Weekly News*. There was a shepherd's job advertised at Stratfield-Saye on the Duke of Wellington's Estate. I rang up and enquired about the job. The boss was a Mr Bucknell and he asked me when I could come for an interview.

'I can be there in an hour,' I said. I had a brand new 650cc Triumph Thunderbird at the time. He asked me over the phone, who he could ring for a reference, and I gave him the number of John Ironmonger, the manager at St. Giles. Georgina and I set off to see this new job. It was a bit sudden after just getting settled in, but I don't take being messed about lightly.

But as I was about to leave, Mathew Cundell came up to the house on the Downs on his horse. He told me to jolly well get back down to the pen and sort out all the problems there were, as he couldn't do it himself. I said, 'Sorry. I've got an interview in an hour at Stratfield-Saye'. He was fuming, and he tried, but in vain, to stand across the front of the gate so I couldn't get out with my bike, but the poor horse didn't like the revs and the sound of the horn. In fact, he almost bucked Mathew Cundell off. He was so wild with me that he was ranting and raving and cursing.

Mr Bucknell at Stratfield-Saye had rung Mr Ironmonger for a verbal reference, and the job was mine before I got there, I think. It was a good house and a good flock of four hundred Scotch Half-Bred ewes, about to start lambing in a week or so. He offered me £5 a week more wages and two shillings per lamb bonus over 100%. Everything was almost ready for lambing to start, in a partly-covered yard. The previous shepherd had died a week earlier of a heart attack. Mr Bucknell liked me. Mr Ironmonger had obviously given me a good reference. Mr Bucknell said, 'The job's yours, if you want it. The lorry will be there on Monday morning to pick you up'.

When I arrived back from the interview, Mr Cundell was there, waiting with his mother, who, in fact, was the real boss. She pleaded politely for me to go back down to the lambing pen, as there were all sorts of problems. I told her that I had found a new job and that I was moving on Monday. But, because Mrs Cundell was such a dear o' lady, and for the sake of the ewes, which I had become attached to over the previous six months, I went back down there. On condition that her arrogant son stayed away, of which she assured me, I sorted all the problems out. There were three hundred ewes in that pen, and it was as though they knew I was leaving. Over the next three days, Friday, Saturday and Sunday, more than two hundred lambed. On the Monday morning Mrs Cundell came and paid me my full wages, plus a further £50. She apologised to me and my wife for all the unnecessary unpleasantness, and said that if there was a chance that I'd change my mind she would love us to stay. But the lorry was coming up the lane, and I said, 'Sorry, it's too late'. The tears started rolling down her face, she shook my hand and said, 'Good luck, and thank you'.

It didn't take long to load the lorry. We never had much furniture then, just the bare essentials, no carpets, only rugs, no luxury fridges, washing machines or deep freezers, not even an electric cooker. The cooking was done in the kitchen range. Later, at this new job, we were gifted with a Rayburn. I think that was why I took the job; it also meant hot, running water.

It was around this time that conditions did improve a little for the general farm workers. Nearly every vacancy included the word 'Rayburn' in the advert, and 'inside toilet', which was a great improvement on the old 'thunder box' up the top of the garden.

I still have some good memories of Aston Tirrold. I played football for the village team and made friends with two great guys, Tony Strange and Sid Webb. We still keep in touch and exchange visits twice a year. They always come down in November when we have our local Dorset Evening at the Trooper and in June when I have the annual auction of bygones and collectables.

We moved to our new job at Stratfield-Saye on the Duke of Wellington's estate. Lambing started immediately and we did well. Mr Bucknell was pleased. We achieved a 178% lambing, which was expected of Scottish half-breeds, crossed Suffolk.

After lambing, when I was out around the farm with the sheep, little things started to go wrong. It wasn't quite so bad as the previous job with the Cundells, but what happened was that there was the boss, Mr Bucknell, his son, about the same age as me, and a farm foreman. Neither of the latter two knew anything about sheep, but would keep giving orders. One day I told them both that I'd come here to work for one boss, not three. As most country and farming people know, all stockmen, if they know their job, are left alone to get on with it.

In the middle of May I mentioned the shearing to the boss. I asked him who would be helping me with pulling out and rolling the wool, which I was quite capable of doing and prepared to do. He said he had a gang coming in to do this.

On the morning they arrived to start, these two scruffy-looking chaps jumped out of an old Landrover. I met them, introduced myself as the new shepherd and asked them roughly how many they wanted for the first day. 'How many have you got,' one of them said, and I told him about four hundred and fifty. 'Oh, we shall do the lot today,' he replied. These ewes were big and in good condition, so I thought, 'They're going to have to go some to do that lot'. I had the first batch ready in the barn for them, so I said, 'While you make a start, I'll go and shed the lambs off and bring in another bunch'. When I got back to the barn, the ewes they had sheared were out in the back yard. And I have never seen so many cuts on shorn sheep as they had. There was blood everywhere, and half the wool was still on them.

I walked straight into the barn, switched the electric off and brought everything to a halt. One of the men looked up and said, 'You've come just right, mate. There's been an electric cut.'

'Cut's bloody right,' I said. 'I've never seen so many cuts on sheep before, so if you think you're going to shear the rest of the flock like that, you're very much mistaken. You can pack up and go right now.'

'Well, how do you expect them to be done?' one asked.

So I switched the power back on, took the hand-piece out of his hand and sheared one exactly how I wanted them done. I don't suppose they thought I could do it, so they said, 'Alright, fair play, mate,' and they started again. I stood over them while they did two or three each, and everything seemed OK – till lunchtime.

After lunch I went to move the ewes round ready to bring them in. I was only gone about twenty minutes, and when I came back, they were at it again. One ewe was cut so badly we had to stitch her up. So I switched the power off again and told them to pack up and really go this time. There was a lot of cussing and swearing, and the way they spoke, they thought I hadn't got a father. They were still cussing as they went out of the yard, and they said, 'We shan't ever come back here again.'

I replied, 'At least you've got one thing right today.'

The foreman said, 'What are we going to do now?'

'I'll be shearing,' I said. 'You will be pulling out and rolling and packing the wool.' So I went home and got my own shearing machine, and away we went. It took an extra day, but at least the job was done properly. From then on, the boss saw me in a different role as shepherd and we got on really well. But his boy and the foreman kind of saw me as a 'big-head', for want of another word, and if they could make things awkward in any way, they would.

We rubbed along until about July, when I had a few days' holiday. I went down to St. Giles to see Mother and Father, and I told them how things were at work and said that I was not really happy. With stock, you've got to be really happy. Shepherding is a wonderful way of life. I always treated the flock as though they were my own, not the farmer's, and most shepherds did and still do.

While I was at home, I met Mr Ironmonger, who told me that the Crichel Estate was going to start a new flock. He offered to put a good word in for me with Mr Peter Crane, the manager, if I was interested. I thought, 'What a wonderful way to get back to dear old Dorset!' So I said, 'Yes, please.'

Peter Crane arranged an interview and we talked for what seemed like hours. We really did sort out how we both wanted long-term commitment. After the last two jobs, I really was looking for that sort of job. Well, that was my destiny for the next twenty years, as it turned out. I saw the sheep arrive, and I saw the flock sold – some of the happiest and one of the saddest days of my life.

4
Downland Days

I arrived at Crichel the last week in July, and four days later, Peter Crane and I flew up to Scotland. We arrived at Turnhouse Edinburgh Airport and were met by an auctioneer and taken to our hotel. The next morning he picked us up. He had arranged for us to go to three different farms over the next two days, and we selected the ewes we wanted from each farm, a total of seven hundred. Transport was all arranged in Scotland, and the ewes all arrived four days later on three huge triple-deck lorries. The amazing thing was, there was only one fatality. They went out onto the famous Crichel Down, and I was the proudest shepherd in Dorset. It was a real challenge, what with my father on the next Estate at Shaftesbury. In his eyes I was still a boy. Each year, as we found our feet, we bought another two hundred, two-tooths, and I was soon overtaking Father's flock. In the next seven or eight years we were up to two thousand ewes and we were one of the largest lamb producers in Dorset.

Peter Crane and Geoffrey Hyde of Lulworth Castle farms started up the company called 'Dorset Quality Lamb Producers' and operated through F.M.C. Uddens at Wimborne. Times were good then and sheep were at their best. We never sold a lamb through the markets in those days. We also sold to Mr Coggan, a large wholesaler at Fareham, near Portsmouth. Some weeks we would be sending off three hundred lambs a week, on one occasion, four hundred, two hundred to F.M.C. and two hundred to

Coggan's. I can tell you, it was quite an impressive sight to see four lorries lined up taking lambs off. At that time, I was getting two bob a lamb bonus, on every lamb sold. Overtime was unheard of. I was paid a good salary and bonus, and you did your job whatever the hours. When I was lambing, it was nothing to do eighteen to twenty hours a day. It's amazing where you get the energy from, but when there are lambs dropping all around you, the adrenaline really flows, along with a cup of tea every now and then.

The heaviest 'drop' of lambs I can recall was when a hundred and eighty ewes lambed in twenty-four hours, and a hundred of those were at night, from seven at night to seven in the morning. There were ewes everywhere. I had to put up twenty or thirty extra single pens and make pens with bales. Everywhere there was a hole I put a ewe and lambs in. Then I started putting two ewes to a pen which had singles, and, before daylight, turned the singles straight into the out-pens, and caught them up to tail and castrate later, as and when we had time. The ewes didn't slow down for days. I stayed at the lambing for a whole week and didn't go home. I just caught a couple of hours' sleep when possible. At the end I was like a zombie, completely knackered, but your enthusiasm for your job kept you going. My mate at the time was Walt Hatcher, a good chap, a hard worker. He would stay up every other night with me to give me a break. It was the quickest lambing I can remember. We'd lambed down a thousand ewes in the first fortnight.

I had a young veterinary student on work experience that year. His name was Andy and he was a good hard worker, so much so that he went on to become a vet. The last I saw or heard of him, he was practising at Long Mead,

Shaftesbury.

Our lambing pens at Crichel were always outside. They had to be, as we moved around to a different site every year, according to the crops and grass rotation. One year we would be at Manswood Bottom, the next over at Tarrant Monkton, the following year at Sheephouse Farm or Cutler's Farm, Deansleaze. With the size of flock we had, we needed over three hundred and fifty acres or more of grass. We stocked at five ewes and lambs to the acre, April to September, then on to roots or the young lays, and part of the flock would go round at least two of the three dairies, clearing up what the cows didn't use, once they were housed.

Most of the fields were fifty acres plus. All of them were then split in half with temporary stock fencing. Then I would alternate each half every four days. It gave the grass a chance to recover, but, more importantly, the sheep weren't peeing on it all the time.

Grass doesn't have to be six to eight inches tall all the time for sheep. The closer to the ground they feed, the better they do. Lush grass only goes straight through them and gives them dirty backsides. That's a good reason for crutching all the ewes before letting them free onto the new young lays in the spring.

A lot of artificial manure was used in those days. I certainly wouldn't have liked to pick up the tab for the cost. And, of course, we had our fair share of magnesium problems. I had a long wheel-base Landrover and there were always a dozen bottles of calcium and magnesium in the cab, and plenty of syringes. I sometimes wondered if non-farming people thought I was a travelling drug addict.

One lambing I had a mate, Les Elford, helping. We had a ewe which had aborted but had plenty of milk. We put her head between two stakes and tried fostering two lambs onto her. The first time was unsuccessful. She beat one poor lamb against the hurdles, crushed its ribs and killed it. So, back she went into the stocks with two fresh lambs for another two days. Virtually the same thing happened, but we did rescue the lambs. Because she was so milky, we tried again. We were determined she was going to take two lambs. On the third try, we had just let her out to see if she had taken the lambs, and, sure enough, she started knocking them about. Les was walking by with a hammer in his hand. He leant over, gently tapped her on the head and said, 'You sod!' He must have caught her in the right (or wrong) place. She fell to the ground unconscious. In fact, I thought she was dead. I said, 'Christ, Les! That was a bit severe. Please don't do that again'. However, her eyes flickered, she shook herself and got up, and you'll never believe this, but it's true, she took those two lambs as though they were her own.

I seriously think that Les thought he had found a new way to foster lambs. I wonder if he ever did it again. Les was so keen on sheep, he moved on and became a shepherd down at Martinstown. I gave him his first collie dog. I always had two or three good dogs. You had to, to move the sheep around a ten thousand acre estate. I was paid £2 a week per dog, feeding allowance, tax free, dare I say, but only for the first two dogs.

With outside pens, snow and heavy rain were our worst enemies, but latterly I had some long tarpaulin cloths that would cover the small, independent pens from the roof to the front hurdles. Each cloth reached along twenty-five coops.

In 1963-64, I spent the entire Boxing Night up on the Downs, walking around the sheep, keeping them moving to keep them on top of the snow. It snowed all night, and if I hadn't done that, a lot of them would have been buried. Sheep are a bit silly when it snows. They just lie there. Many times I've dug out ewes and lambs. At daybreak the snow eased off a little and the sheep were standing on solid snow, about a foot thick. We'd had about eighteen inches of snow that night and it had drifted up across to where we were. If you look at sheep in a field, they will always go to the highest point for the night's sleep. When it came to daylight, I couldn't get home myself. Manswood Hill was solid. I had to wait until our tractors and snowploughs came through. Peter Crane was good in those sorts of circumstances. He would always make sure there was access to the sheep and dairies for feeding. When there was snow around, I always made sure they had plenty of hay and extra cake. Water wasn't so important. Sheep will eat or lick snow if they're thirsty.

The first two years at Crichel, I taught Arthur Langford and Henry Hamblin to shear, and the three of us would manage, but once we got over a thousand ewes, we decided it was quicker to get a gang in.

Sadly, it was about this time that my marriage with Georgina broke up. The children were all at school, we were both working very long hours and didn't see as much of each other as we ought to have done. But, after all the little upsets that happen in divorces, the dust settled. The good thing is we have all remained good friends, which, of course, was good for the children's sake. We still exchange birthday cards and Christmas presents and on special occasions we have a meal together.

After thirteen years I got married again, to Sue, my present wife. We have been married for fourteen years. For several years she worked alongside me as a shepherdess.

Both Georgina and Sue are hard-working ladies, and I count myself very lucky to have shared a great part of my life with two wonderful women.

During the time I was at Crichel, we made five appearances on television on the 'Out of Town' programme with Jack Hargreaves – lambing, shearing, dipping and selecting the ewes and tups for the next year. The fifth programme was when I was made redundant. I had to sell my collection of bygones. The sale was held at Tarrant Monkton, behind the Langton Arms pub. I had stationary engines by the score, four-wheeled wagons, vintage tractors, root pulpers, a cider press and jars. You name it, it was there, even an old Rover 70 saloon car. But the good Lord was not on my side that day. It poured torrents all through the sale. I was amazed that the TV cameraman stuck it out, but he did have a very large umbrella.

Jack and I became good friends during those years. I also used to let him have unusual items for the end of each programme, when he would ask, 'What is it?' Nine times out of ten, we both knew what the items were, but he did it to get viewers' response and feedback. Jack followed us to the Trooper. He was here every Tuesday for lunch.

One day he said, 'I know what I'll do. We'll get the five programmes we made at Crichel and do a new piece on the Trooper. We'll do a small documentary and call it "The Life of Shepherd to a Publican". That will put you on the map.' But it wasn't to be. He died about a month later, but his photo still hangs in the bar, above where he always sat. It was his dying wish that we should succeed and, thankfully, that wish has come true. We are busier now.

Jack Hargreaves was good company. We had a lot in common, especially about the countryside. He loved it, so much so that his ashes are scattered on the side of the hill on Bullbarrow, looking out over Belchalwell, where he last lived. Although Jack was from Yorkshire, he loved Dorset. Unless you've read Jack's book, *Out of Town*, there aren't many people who know that he was a vet, and then went to Fleet Street for many years before going into television.

Jack had a sixth sense, and he knew whether people were genuine or not. He could tell straight away if certain people wanted to talk to him and listen to his stories, or whether they just wanted to be seen with him, so that they could go away and say 'I've spoken to Jack Hargreaves', been there, done that kind of attitude. That's when he would cut people a bit short. It wasn't exactly rude. He told me that the most common approach was, 'Hello, Mr Hargreaves. I saw you on telly last night'. Then it would be the next question or remark that was important to him, and would decide whether he would carry on the conversation or not. Most people thought that because they had seen something on television the night before, Jack would remember straight away what they were on about. Most of his programmes were made at least a year earlier. Whether it's true or not, and I have no reason to doubt it, he told me that he never watched himself on television.

Despite what anyone says about him, he was amongst my closest friends. He encouraged me to put my father's bells on the ewes, when we were on the Downs. It's the most wonderful sound to any old shepherd. You can tell by the sound whether the flock is grazing peacefully or being harassed by a dog or just breaking out of the folds. Sometimes it was even possible to forecast by the sound, and with incredible accuracy, the next day's weather and which way the wind was blowing.

My two daughters, Belinda and Sandra, were always willing to help me. They spent a lot of time with the sheep, and not because I made them. They were as keen as I was. They could work the dogs, move electric fences, shed lambs through the handling pens, even age the ewes by the number of teeth they had. Sheep throw up two main teeth every year until they are full-mouthed, with eight teeth. The process takes four years. You will never hear shepherds refer to their ewes as one-year or two-year-olds. It is always 'hogs' until they are eighteen months old. Then they are two-tooths, four-tooths, six-tooths and full-mouthed, then draft ewes and regular draft. It's only after that they are kept in the flock, if they retain a good set of teeth.

Ewes are very reliant on their teeth, especially if they feed on root crops. The next age referral is broken-mouthed, and that's when they lose two or three teeth, but can still survive. When they get down to that stage, it's better to have none than just one or two teeth. Over the years, if a ewe was still in good condition and prolific, I have removed the teeth for her, but it was not a good policy to keep too many old ewes in a big flock. It cost no more to keep a young one than an old one. As they get older they need more attention and seem to develop more problems. The longest time I ever kept a ewe was twelve years. She was known as 'O' Granny', and she was a natural leader, always up front with the bell on. She produced nearly thirty lambs, never ever had less than twins, and one year, had quads. With her in the flock, I used to say I could move a flock through London. She would follow you anywhere.

My daughters loved it at lambing time. They sat up with me at nights on weekends or on half-terms, and were a great help with weak or orphan lambs, or suckling lambs off the milky ewes. I would never bottle-feed a lamb if I could get enough milk from another ewe. If you fed them artificially for three or four days it was harder to get them back onto a ewe. If I had a really good old milky ewe, or one with enlarged teats, I would keep her around in the pen for up to a week or ten days, or until another one came along. I would keep one of that sort around all the time. It was far easier and more natural than boiling a kettle.

I'd be the first to say my patience was at breaking point during lambing time. I wanted everything to be just right. Sometimes I would need extra help from other farm-hands, for example, if it was a wet night, if it was snowing, if there were ewes and lambs to move on or extra littering to do.

Peter Crane and I would often have words, sometimes if he didn't send men when I wanted them. I believe I gave in my notice to him at least eight times, but he never took any notice of it. He knew I was hyped up and always said afterwards, 'When you're like that, I know the job's being done properly'. I must admit he was pretty good and generous with help when I needed it. In return, when the shepherding was quieter, during harvest time, I would help him. I relieved the three combine drivers twice a day, at dinner and tea times, half an hour each. It meant that I was combining three hours a day, and it was made easy because I had a Landrover and could get from one to the other pretty quickly. The drivers had somewhere to sit in comfort, and I enjoyed doing it. If one driver was away, I would drive all day and Sue would take over as shepherdess. Sue, my wife, worked full-time with the sheep on Crichel. We managed together, and had help at shearing, dipping and lambing times only. She had her own dog, Lazro. He was one of the best we ever had.

Shepherds usually tell tall stories about their dogs. I remember a shepherd at Mr Tory's at Shapwick telling my father that he had a dog that could tell him if a ewe had fly-strike and would catch the ewe and hold her till he got there. My father, never short of a reply, said he never had fly-strike in his ewes because his dog would sit in the gateway to the field all day and catch the bluebottle flies as they came through the gate.

'Did 'er now,' said the shepherd, 'and what happened when thees went home?'

'We shut the gate,' said Father.

Another story I recall Father telling was when he was at Breamore with the Hampshire Down Pedigrees. In those days they would show the sheep, and they were coloured with a yellowish-orange reddle powder. Only the Hampshire Downs did this, and, at the Royal Show one year, Prince Philip came round and inspected the sheep. He asked Father how the sheep got that colour. Father's ready answer was, 'We feed them on oranges.' Obviously, he told him why afterwards. I had the privilege of shaking hands with the Prince as we were holding the rams out for him to inspect. I also rubbed shoulders with Prince Charles and took pheasants from him when he shot on the Crichel Estate. Sometimes I helped on the game cart and picked up the back-guns in my Landrover.

The Head Keeper, Ernie Langdon, asked if he could move to a smaller place, which he did, and I was offered his big house. I'd got three children by now. My son, Roland, had arrived, so we needed a larger place. I couldn't believe my luck when Peter Crane offered me the house. It was called 'The Cloisters', and it had a friendly ghost. It also had some top class kennels for my dogs.

It was while I was at Crichel that I started making walking sticks. An old friend at Sixpenny Handley, Billy Day, influenced me, and I've been at it ever since. It's a pleasant hobby. We have a stick dressers' meeting twice a year in the skittle alley.

Lunch in one hand, lamb in the other. Lambing time in 1980
at Manswood Bottom on the Crichel Estate.

I've so far built up three collections of rural bygones, and here I am with an old shepherding hut I found at Tisbury.

A Petter Oil Stationary Engine, 1980. Looking on is Steve Oliver of the Bournemouth & Poole Preservation Club.

The Deer Park Inn, Lydlinch, near Sturminster Newton, where Sue and I spent four years behind the bar. The pub is now closed.

My niece, Nicky Jessie, giving a shearing demonstration at the Courtyard Craft Centre, Lytchett Minster, whilst I keep a watchful eye from the background.

Two views of The Trooper Inn, Stourton Caundle, our home for the last eight years. The upper photograph is of the inn in the early 1900s. The building has been an inn since about 1670, changing its name from the Catherine Wheel during the Napoleonic Wars.

Me with a small section of my collection of rural bygones in the Museum that means so much to me at the rear of The Trooper.

Me sitting proudly on the very last sheep pen to be removed from
Sturminster Newton Market when it closed in 1997,
and now part of my Museum Collection.

My three children, Sandra, Belinda and Roland, at the
Castleman Hotel, Chettle, in 1999.

Sue and I with the 'Spring Pub of the Year Award' from the
Campaign for Real Ale (CAMRA) in 1999.

One year, while at Crichel, I had a busman's holiday. I joined Billy Kinghorn's shearing gang and went over to the Isle of Arran, shearing. That was an experience I shall never forget, for it was a totally different way of shepherding.

We arrived at one farm at about half-past seven in the morning. There were five of us in the gang, and fourteen hundred sheep to shear. We wanted to finish them in a day, so an early start was required. The farmer greeted us on arrival. 'Right,' he said, 'Go on indoors. Mother's got breakfast on for 'ee all. I'm just going to get the sheep down off the mountains.'

I will always remember it. I looked around and could see for at least a two-mile radius of his farm, surrounded by mountains, which must have been three thousand feet above sea level. I couldn't even see a sheep. He had four Collie dogs. He cast two to the left and the others to the right. And there we were, sitting in his large kitchen eating the biggest breakfast I've ever had. About half an hour later, these sheep started to appear off the top of the mountains. It was well over an hour before the first ewes arrived into the shearing shed. The last ones arrived about another hour after we had started shearing. The majority of them sheared well, until I had one that had been missed the previous year, so she had a 'double coat'. It was so matted together that it was a job to get under it with the shears. When I did eventually get it off I had a ready-made carpet.

We eventually finished the flock at about eight o'clock in the evening. We were dying for a pint and the farmer said, 'Go on indoors. Have a wash and a brush-up. Mother's got supper for 'ee all'. You've never seen so much food in your life – a big leg of venison, a leg of lamb and the equivalent of a quarter truckle of cheese. There was wine by the bottle, and whisky galore. We were on Arran for ten days and were invited to parties on at least six nights. We were treated like royalty. They love their music and singing, and to those farmers, only having sheep as an income, it was a kind of Harvest Supper when the sheep were all nice and cleanly sheared.

5

Wiltshire Interlude

Eventually the running of Crichel Estate was handed over to new land agents. Two years later the flock was sold and I was made redundant. I could have stayed as a tractor driver, but sheep were in my blood. I was offered a job at Lawn Farm, Tisbury, as Working Farm Manager. It was a two hundred and fifty acre sheep, corn and grass seed farm, owned by Major Kenny-Herbert. What a gentleman he was! He had two hundred mule ewes, and grew about sixty acres of grass seed, which worked well and combined with the sheep being able to have the second-year lays. I did the combining, ploughing and drilling. I had to take a spraying course, and quickly learnt to use the baler. The Major also had fifty acres of steep ground, mainly covered in blackthorn and brambles. Richard, my stepson, and I took it into our hands to clear these slopes. It took over a year, but we cleared the lot, so it meant we could increase the flock. That was my main objective. Eventually we were up to four hundred.

The farm was divided by its steep valley. The Major lived at Lawn Farm and I lived at Weavelands Farm. It worked out the easiest to have two hundred ewes on each farm, from the grazing point of view. We would put them together at tupping time. Then the first two hundred and fifty or so that went to tup would be brought to Weavelands, and the others to Lawn. If any returned to the ram, they would go back as well. That way, they were split ready for lambing. We had a lambing shed on both farms.

It was a clean farm, almost wild oat free. All our corn was grown for seed, under contract, winter wheat and spring barley, for Wiltshire Farmers Co. at Melksham. They would pay an extra £10 premium per ton. It was seldom we were under three ton per acre of wheat. What few wild oats were there, we would rogue. Their crop inspector would come down two or three times. He would kneel down with a pair of binoculars, each side of the field, to see if any wild oats were apparent. At harvest time, he would take two or three seven-pound bag samples back with him for inspection. We never ever had any rejected, and there were far fewer fertilizers and sprays used then than today.

Drying of the corn was kept to a minimum, as over-drying it would affect germination. A sample test for that was taken before it was picked up from the farm. A huge built-in air blower was used for under-floor drying and conditioning. Each bin held a hundred tons, and if there was any doubt about one of them, we would turn on a small amount of heat. We had our own simple way of testing it for moisture. After about ten minutes we would lay a pane of glass on top of the bin of corn, and if a film of condensation appeared, we would leave the blower on for a while.

The Major had another way to test the airflow. He always wore a silk cravat and he would take it off and lay it on top of the corn. If the airflow was good, the cravat would hover about an inch above the corn. I never had a cravat, so I would do the same sort of thing with a page from a daily paper. If sometimes it didn't hover when we thought it should, we would put it down to the weight of the rubbish on the page.

The o' Major was a wonderful man to work for and very appreciative. If, during any part of the year, he thought you had worked hard, or achieved something good, there would be a little bonus in your wage packet. This could happen possibly seven or eight times a year. It was nearly always a tenner, and he always gave me £100 bonus extra at haymaking, harvest, as a Christmas present and at lambing time. He was a generous man. To his close friends, he was known as 'Teddy', but always 'Major' to me. Richard, my stepson eventually, came on and worked there when Jim Burbidge left. We ran it on our own for four and a half years. If a third man was needed the Major would roll up his sleeves and do his bit. We dreaded him volunteering to harrow-in behind the drill. You could guarantee there would be some fencing to do afterwards.

One particular day he was harrowing in Reservoir Field, and he couldn't go backwards or forwards, he was so far into the fence. He hitched off the tractor and came across to me and said, 'Larry, You'd better take the fore loader up. I've had a little mishap, and could you please finish the field, I've a meeting to go to'. It usually was a meeting, but a race meeting on the telly, with a Scotch in his hand. He loved a little tipple.

Unfortunately, we parted company over a difference of opinion. He had a brainstorm one day, came up the field and said he was going to run the farm on a different strategy. He was going to reduce the ewes to two hundred, rent out the steep hangings and have low input and lower output. I couldn't come to terms with that. We had all the machinery and all the facilities. It was a lovely farm, and every year we made a good profit. He would show me when we had a meeting of costs and balance accounts, when we discussed next year's planning. He told me, and I quote, 'I don't need to make all this money'. He could see little point in adding to the corn mountains developing in the country.

We are still good friends. We parted amicably. Three years later, he packed up farming and rents it out to two other farmers in Tisbury.

During the time I was with Major Kenny-Herbert I started collecting old farming bygones again, and had several sheds full, which meant having a second auction when I left. It broke my heart to see it all go under the hammer.

While searching for a permanent job, I helped out at the Shire Horse Centre at Teffont near Salisbury. I did the sheep dog demonstrations on Saturdays and Sundays, helped with the Shires and also helped the wheelwright bonding the large wooden cartwheels. Another weekend we had a threshing demonstration. Two ricks were put through with a reed comber bundling the straw for local thatchers. John Webb had some lovely Shire horses there, but, unfortunately, it never really did get off the ground. It closed after about two years and is now, I believe, a riding school for the disabled.

During my four and a half years at Weavelands farm, I made friends with Auriol and Robin Biddle. Auriol paints milk churns and other metal ware. She turns them into wonderful, sought-after gems. Robin and I are rivals at collecting bygones and memorabilia, but we do buy for each other at car-boot sales and auctions. Robin's specialities are scales. I collect almost everything. At present I have seven hundred ashtrays, eighty sheep and cow-bells, a hundred old irons, a hundred and fifty pen-knives, seventy vermin traps, twenty shepherds' crooks, thirteen different root pulpers and chaff cutters, two shepherds' huts and a whole museum of agricultural and country bygones – all of which is starting to attract quite a few people to the Trooper.

6

From Shepherd to Publican

I applied for several shepherding jobs without success, because no farmer seemed to want you after you were fifty years old and at your best. Each answer was, 'Sorry, I'm looking for someone between twenty-five and thirty years old'. One Tuesday afternoon, I arrived home from Salisbury market and my wife, Sue, said to me, 'I've applied for a job in *The Blackmore Vale Magazine*. We've got an interview tomorrow at one o'clock'. She showed me the advertisement and I couldn't believe what I was reading. It was for 'a young couple' to manage a small country pub, the Deer Park, at Lydlinch, about ten miles from Sherborne. I said, 'Have you disclosed our ages. It says he wants "a young couple"?'

The next day, I made myself look as young as possible, as one would. I put on a tie for the first time in about two years. We arrived at the Deer Park at a quarter to one, and there stood an old friend of mine, Peter Amey. I had no idea he had the pub, and he certainly didn't realise I was the person applying for the job. Sue obviously hadn't said who we were, and he thought we had just called in for a drink. We were talking generally and he mentioned that he had a couple coming for an interview at one clock, so he would be leaving us to go into the other bar. I said, 'Well, we had better come with you. We are that couple'. He only ever knew me as a shepherd, but he knew that Sue had a lot of barmaid and stewardess experience. We talked at length and he said, 'Well, I suppose I can teach you, but I have

three other couples to interview yet, in the next two days'.
We left, knowing we had no chance. When we got home at
four o'clock, the phone was ringing. Sue answered, and it
was Peter Amey. He said, 'How soon can you be here? The
job's yours'.

Taking the job meant selling my own small flock of a
hundred mule ewe lambs, which I was running on to be
sold the following September at Wilton Sheep Fair, as
breeding two-tooth ewes. I had acquired half of these ewe
lambs by doing a local farmer's night's lambing for him the
previous March. Instead of money, I had the pick of the ewe
lambs. I bought the other half from him at what would
have been killing price for fat lambs. Each week I would
give him a hand to weigh off his lambs and pick out what I
wanted. I had a matching hundred lambs, like peas in a
pod. I'd only just recently made up my mind to run my own
flock and go contract shepherding.

I sold the sheep at Sturminster Newton Market, and the
following week, moved to the Deer Park pub at Lydlinch.
Most 'Darzet' people would more likely remember it as the
Three Boars Inn (the Three Pigs). It was the first week of
December, 1987, with Christmas looming up. I had to learn
pretty fast how to pull a good pint, but I had one of the best
tutors there was in Peter Amey. He knew 'every trick of the
trade', to coin a phrase. He told me never ever to tamper
with the top shelf, meaning watering down the clear spirits
like gin and vodka. 'Your whole reputation is at stake,' he
said. The weights and measures can drop in on you any
time they wish, and they still do, about once a year.

His advice was, 'Always clean your pipes once a week to
keep the beer at its best, always be civil to customers, but
don't take any rubbish from them'. And that was good,
coming from Peter because he could be so rude to

customers, in the nicest possible way, that only he could get away with it. Most people knew this and would come back for more. They loved it, and so did Peter. He was always playing tricks on people, and 'setting them up'. Once I will never forget, a customer came in with a lovely blue willow-pattern meat dish. He asked if Peter thought he'd been ripped off at £40. Peter had a good look at it in a brighter light in the kitchen. He went through, picked up one of our own identical plates and dropped it on the tiled floor, smashing it to pieces. I'll never forget the poor chap's face. Peter returned and said, 'How much did you say you paid for it?'

The man replied, 'Whatever it was, you're going to have to pay me for it'.

Peter kept this charade up for about twenty minutes, winding this poor bloke up. That was typical of Peter. We had some great times while we were there for four years with him, as his managers.

It's a Dorset tradition to give your real regulars a free drink on Christmas Day. Peter said, 'Never give them the first drink. Let 'um buy the first and give 'um the next, 'cos sometimes they'll have just one and "bugger off" to the next pub, and do the same'. And, believe it or not, there are people who do that. We had a customer who bragged about going to four or five local pubs and never spent a penny. And I still do that at the Trooper, unless it's my real regulars, who I know are there to stay. Then sometimes I'll give 'um two. We once had a Londoner come to stay at the Deer Park, and, during the course of the evening, he reckoned that he was a connoisseur of whiskies. Peter challenged him. He said, 'I'll put one of each of our whiskies in a glass, and if you can name each one correctly, you can have them free, on the house, or you pay me double if you're wrong.' At the time, we had six different ones on the shelf. So, this chap went to the toilet, and we put up six glasses. When he came back, he endeavoured to tell us the whiskies, one by one. After supping them all, he said, 'How many have I got correct?' We said, 'One, the Famous Grouse'.

He said, 'Yes. That's the first glass. I never fail on that one'.

Peter answered, 'Well, you have this time, because they are all Grouse'.

Peter always enjoyed a 'spoof' with friends. It's a game played with as many people as you like, but best with just four or five. Each holds up to three coins, or as few as none, in his hand, and the others have to guess the total being held. The last one out buys the round. Peter loved it so much, he played by proxy, over the phone, while in bed recovering from 'flu. He had to declare his hand first each time, and would trust me to see fair play with the others, who were, if my memory serves me correctly, the Frost brothers, from Bagber, and John Harris.

Sadly, our time at the Deer Park came to an end. Peter told me he had sold the pub and he gave us a fortnight's notice. So, after four and a half years with Peter, we were made redundant again. We didn't find a suitable job immediately, so he let us have the little cottage next door, until we got ourselves sorted out.

Trying for other suitable jobs wasn't easy. My age was against me even more this time. Going back to full time shepherding was out of the question. After years of handling wet sheep and walking through wet grass osteo-arthritis had taken its toll on my knees. I was out of work for about three weeks, and suddenly knew what it felt like to be unemployed and like a fish out of water.

Luck was on our side. Mike and Linda Wise, from the Courtyard Craft Centre at Lytchett Minster, heard that we were looking for a job and asked us to join them as managers. So we took up their offer and I was 'in clover' once again. Crafts are close to my heart, and I had fifteen units to look after. We all worked well together. Each weekend I ran different events to attract customers, not only to the craft units, but also to the restaurant, where Sue was manageress. They uusually consisted of such things as displayes of vintage cars and motor-cycles, threshing, thatching, steam engines and sheep-shearing demonstrations.

After eighteen months our time there came to end, and once again we faced a less than certain future. It was then that 'lady luck' finally took a hand. One Monday morning the phone rang. It was Pat Davison, the landlady of The Trooper Inn, Stourton Caundle, a quiet village buried in the heart of the Blackmore Vale. That phone call was to change our lives.

7

The Trooper Inn

Pat Davison's Monday morning phone call to Sue came like a bolt out of the blue. Pat said that she was seriously thinking of giving up The Trooper Inn. She wanted to know if we would be interested, as she thought we would be the ideal couple for it. She was not going to sell to 'any o' body'. She wanted a certain type of person, who would get on with her customers.

We knew each other from our days at the Deer Park. She said she had thought long and hard about who she would like to take it. We agreed to meet at the Crown Hotel in Blandford to talk it through over lunch. She was the most helpful person, and so determined that we would have it, that she'd come along armed with four different proposals.

The main proposal was to sell The Trooper, the next was to manage it for a while for her, so that we could get the feel of it, the third was to go into partnership with her, and the final one was to lease it for three years, with the option to buy at the end or lease it for another three years. We eventually took the last option, agreed terms and everything, and decided on a date, which was September 6th, 1993. That date was very important to Pat. It meant she had been there seven years to the day.

After some serious thinking, I had worked out that if we leased The Trooper for two consecutive periods of three years, our time would have been up on September 6th, 1999, and I was determined to be its landlord at the turn of the century. In case Pat pulled the mat from under us, we decided to buy after the first three years. I've never once regretted it. It's one of the best pubs in Dorset. I can't think of one I would swap it for. It's unique, and so are most of the customers

The Trooper is not the sort of pub to have if you want to get rich, but if, like me, you're satisfied with a reasonable living, good friends and being able to pay your way, then it's the place for you. We are not in competition with either of the pubs around us. In fact, if people come in and want Sunday lunches, I direct them to Hugh at the White Hart in Bishop's Caundle, or to Andy at the Green Man in King's Stag, not necessarily in that order. It depends who's paying the best commission. At the moment, they are both paying the same – nothing!

We have ten regular skittle teams and two darts teams, and without them we couldn't survive. We are grateful to them all. I don't skittle often, but I do like a game of darts: Tuesday is my darts night out with 'the boys'.

The reason we are grateful to the sports' teams, and I'm sorry to have to say this, is that of the three hundred plus people living in the village, only thirty-two are what we call regulars, who come in at least once a week. The village has lost its school, chapel, shop and post office, and it would be a pity to lose the pub.

I'm sure that if I applied for a change of use for The Trooper, there would soon be a petition around with three hundred signatures to stop it. It happened at Lydlinch with the Deer Park, though no number of names could save it. It's a question of 'use it or lose it', whether it's a pub, a shop or a market. In the 1940's to 1960's we would see whole families in the village, outside the local pub on a summer Saturday or Sunday evening, and there wasn't the money around then as there is now. I suppose there were not so many motor cars either.

Stourton Caundle is one of the prettiest villages in Dorset, and that's why people like to come here from London and other cities to retire. Sadly, it often seems that they have become used to a different kind of place to drink in, such as a wine bar. Happily, this doesn't apply to those who've come to live in the village. Many love it, the peace of the countryside, the gentler pace of country life. Some say it's like a time warp, an opportunity to go back to quality village life.

Now that the school has vanished, and the post office and village shop are closed, the pub is the only everyday meeting point in the village. It isn't because I'm a publican that I say this. I'd love to see a village post office and shop in Stourton Caundle again, used every day and well supported by the community. But so often I meet people in the village, some of whom still have the old prejudices about being seen going into a pub, others who have their wines delivered to the door and drink at home. I say, 'I haven't seen you at the pub,' and they reply, 'Oh, we don't drink'.

But the world of the pub is something special. A small sherry and a chat at the bar amongst friends does the power of good at lunchtime, and 'puts the world to rights'. I'm sure there's more sense talked in pubs than in the Houses of Parliament. There's not so much backbiting and, what's more people wait for each other to have their say before butting in. It would do the likes of Tony Blair good to be in The Trooper some nights, having a drink and listening to some of the old farming stalwarts, like Dave Harris, Henry Paull, John Waltham, Rob Selway – and many more who come to the pub from around the Blackmore Vale. They say that today they spend more time with a pen rather than a prong, in their hand, filling in forms for people who've never set foot on a farm. Today there is far too much interference by the Government: farmers being told what to grow or what not to grow, subsidies, quotas – it's all out of control, and seldom to the farmers' benefit.

I honestly believe that the reason the Government wants to make it hard for rural places like pubs, shops and post offices to make a small living, is because that's where village people meet and talk about them. Their ears must be burning all day, every day. The only interest Government ministers have in the countryside is in buying their second homes to retreat to at weekends. They bring their own food and drink in the boot of their cars, spend nothing in the countryside, and go home again on Sunday evening.

We love the country all week, all our lives. That's why we live in it. Why do they make things worse all the time? Leave the farmers alone. We don't need their stupid ideas flowing over into the countryside. We love the local bits of gossip, the chitchat, while waiting to be served. In the towns and cities, people don't even know their next-door neighbour, let alone the person next to them in the queue, and, what's more, they don't care either.

But there is another side to this. I put a lot of the blame on the local villagers, who go off into the towns and support the supermarkets. Stop it! Support your own little village amenities. It's self-destruction. Boycott the supermarkets. Don't go there just because you can save twenty pence at the counter. Stop and think! It takes twenty-five pence to get there, and while you're there you buy their loss leaders and 'close to sell-by date' products, because they're down three pence. The housewives, or, more so, the house-husbands, are brainwashed into buying all this rubbish, helping them to clear the shelves, ready for some of the weekenders, down from London, to buy fresh.

Help your local shops. If we all did that, perhaps they could do more special offers. Myself, I don't do any shopping. If I had my way, I would still have daily roundsmen calling, like the baker and butcher. I really admire Dick 'the fish' Curtis, still coming round the villages each week. Long may he continue. He's always smiling, and always has a story to tell, come rain or shine.

Have we really made progress in the last two decades, with our supermarkets, form filling and quotas? Twenty years ago, when I was farming, life was simpler. Farmers never grew or produced what they couldn't sell. It all took care of itself. I dread to think of all the paperwork I would have had when I was working on Crichel Estate with over two thousand breeding ewes.

A couple of years ago, I was sweeping up outside The Trooper, and the water flowing in the brook was white. Apparently the farmer had told the dairyman to pull the plug on the tank. 'Let it go,' he said, 'we are over-producing anyway. We're above our quotas and we'll be fined'. But that's enough of that. I've said enough . . .

At one time The Trooper was called the Catherine Wheel, but at the time of the Napoleonic Wars, in the early nineteenth century, the name was changed. It was probably about then, in honour of the Duke of Wellington, that the road to Sturminster Newton was called Waterloo Lane.

Since being here we've made some wonderful friends. We tend to look upon Dave Harris as the evenings' entertainer. He's always got a story to tell. Monday was his best night, when he would get back from Stur. Market. Sometimes I would go with him, and other farmers would come up to him and say, 'Yer, Dave, 'as y' 'eard this 'un?' And whether he had or not, he would listen politely. There are a lot of people around Dorset who have had a jolly good evening with him. He is always being asked to be an after-dinner speaker, and not only in Dorset.

I once heard him speak to the Wiltshire Old Farmers at Melksham. A farmer put us up for the night. Our wives, Ann and Sue, were with us, and Dave's wife, Ann, and I happened to go down together in the morning. We sat at the table chatting, waiting for Sue and Dave to appear. Well, it was clear this farmer had us mixed up as couples, so we added to the confusion, saying what was said in bed the previous night. By the time we'd finished breakfast he thought we'd had a swap around. We did let on before we left, much to his relief, and more so to the relief of his dear wife.

As I'm a collector of old bygones, it's a well-known fact that I can't resist looking in skips. Many's the time the girls will tell Dave to drive on past a pub if there's a skip in the car park. Dave teases them and says, 'We will take a trailer next year', and Ann's response is, 'You can blooming well go on your own, then!'

Henry Paull, he's another that comes in regularly. He's a bit different from Dave, but he'll bend over backwards to help someone. We first met at a tug-of-war competition at a pub, now closed, called the Bugle Horn, at Tarrant Gunville. He's the sort of chap 'once met, never forgotten'. Sadly, he's just retired from farming, possibly a wise move, considering its state today.

Another farmer I always like to see come in is John Waltham, from Purse Caundle. He'll sing a song at the drop of a hat, and he's also the local wassailing man. According to John, there are several ways to ensure that an apple tree is fruitful – tapping the butt of the tree with sticks, dipping the branches in wooden buckets of cider and asking them to produce more apples the following year, pouring cider round the roots of the tree to feed and nourish it, dancing round the tree to make it feel happy and wanted, making a lot of noise to frighten evil spirits away and, if possible, burying a dead wren under the tree. The wren was known to be fiery and would keep away other birds and evil spirits.

Another entertainer is little Jimmy Eeles. After a couple of bacardis, he can coax a tune out of a tin tray, or a pair of tin snips. The next morning, put a welder in his hand and you've got a genius. He can make anything, from a poker to a spiral staircase: next time you're passing The Trooper, look for the unusual gate he made for the entrance to the car park.

Friday night at the Trooper is my favourite time, when the cream of the spoofers, Chris Vining, Phil Burge, Dave Harris and Henry Paull are in. For Friday lunch we have in 'the last of the summer wine', Phil Kendell, Sam Crane and Harry Corbin, and 'the three ladies', Mary, Stella and Lesley, six lovely people, who all enjoy a bit of banter, with Les Bushell as the co-ordinator.

Once two fishermen from London came into the inn, boasting of the big fish they had caught the day before in the River Stour at Blandford. Harry Corbin sat listening. Then he said, 'Thees 'asn't caught the longest one yet'.

'How long is he?' one of them asked.

'I don't know exactly,' Harry replied, 'but I know he has to wait for the Stour to flood each year to be able to turn round'.

8
Country Ways

What gives me the greatest pleasure of all here at the pub, surrounded by all my 'junk', as Sue calls it, is when older people stop and talk about the things they see, and reminisce. They say things like, 'Cor blimey, I remember using one o' they things forty years ago', or sometimes, 'It's blooming donkey years ago I last seed one o' they'. I listen intently when a grandfather is telling his grandson about it, and explaining how to use it, or what it is. And it's not only grandfathers.

It's amazing how many grans have used them and know what most of them are for. I know the old ladies worked a damned sight harder fifty years ago than their daughters and granddaughters do today. Many would work alongside their husbands all day, hoeing, haymaking and milking by hand. I can even remember my gran and mother going into the cornfield, after the binder, gleaning, picking up the odd ears of corn, taking them home, rubbing them out by hand, grinding them with a pestle and mortar and making their own flour for bread.

In those days, nothing was wasted. After the sheaves had all been picked up off the field with horses and carts, I helped my father push the old chicken house on wheels out into the cornfields to let the hens clean up any odd grains of corn. We'd push them on about thirty yards each night. They used to love that, scratching about on fresh ground, but it wasn't long before the carters and horses would be out with the plough, to turn the stubble under.

There'd be another two horses behind with the press, which was used a lot in the old days. It was also put to work when old pastures were ploughed up. It made the drill for the seed to be broadcast by hand with a seed lip or a seed fiddle. It was then harrowed to cover it in. Where the seed had rolled down into the press marks, it would come up all in a line, like it does today with a precision root drill costing over two thousand pounds. It's what's known as 'progress', but is it all really necessary? The end product is still the same as it was a hundred years ago, and set-aside wasn't heard of.

We did have fallow ground, but that was for a reason, to clean it during the summer of couch. Now it's sprayed today, at a hell of a cost. So who were the cleverest farmers, the old ones or the modern ones? I know, and so do most of you. It's self-explanatory when you look in *The Western Gazette* every week and see all the farms up for sale – specially in the wake of this year's terrible outbreak of Foot and Mouth disease.

Charlock is a weed which is always mentioned on the spray cans, but the odd bit here and there was never a great problem. It seldom seeded to any great proportion. Yellow-hammers and other small birds ate the seed. But how many yellow-hammers and skylarks do we see today? Hardly any. I can never understand why all the countryside 'antis' don't try harder with that side of things, instead of worrying about a fox or two being hunted. Foxes are predators anyway. Docks! They weren't that big a problem to a farmer. Some farmers would use a dock-lifter as a walking stick, and dig the odd one out, or cut them off with a horse-drawn mower, before they went to seed. Charlock and dock will be on this planet as long as humans have 'holes' in their trousers, to put it politely. Charlock seeds were found fifty feet down in the ground, years ago, when wells were dug. They can stay dormant for years and years. Thistles are another weed which hurts no one, unless, of course, you pick it. Finches would feed off them, and butterflies loved them. I once had a donkey, and he loved the heads as well.

But donkeys aren't sheep, and as you can imagine most of my memories are about sheep, since they've been such an important part of my life.

With pedigree Hampshire Downs the rams were not supposed to be introduced to the ewes before 6th August, which meant starting lambing on 1st January, but it was a well-known fact that a certain breeder, who was winning all the prizes, started at least fourteen days earlier. Of course, his lambs were that much more mature than those of the rest of us. At the Royal Show, Father had a real topping ram, well worthy of winning the championship. The judge put our ram in first place to start off with, but then moved the other breeder's up front and put ours second. After letting them run together, he put ours back in first. Finally, he changed his mind again, and we finished second. When we were putting them back in the pens, which were next to each other, Father's rival said, 'I thought you were going to beat me today'.

Father replied, 'If mine had had some Christmas pudding like yours did, he would 'ave done'.

The other breeder didn't reply to that. He knew what Father meant – that they were born early, before Christmas. To rub salt into the wound, the judge came to Father after all the judging, and said, 'We didn't want to be the first to stand him down'. That ram of his had won at the Oxford Show and the Royal Bath and West, or Southern Counties, as it was called then. He hadn't been beaten.

We took the same ram to Britford Sheep Fair the following August. He topped the sale price at five hundred guineas, and who bought it? – the judge.

The Britford Sheep Fair stopped just after that. I remember that the farm on which the fair was held always reckoned to have a corn rick built before the sale day. The farmer and his men would pride themselves on that achievement, for all to see. The sale eventually moved to Wilton, and I believe the first sale of the four held there each year is still called 'the Old Britford Fair'.

The first time I went to Wilton with Father, as a boy, was about 1945 to 46. The person I always remember was the smartly-dressed Mr John Jefferies, with his bowler hat and black boots and gaiters. At one sale, he gave me a shilling for helping the drovers to pen the sheep. That was good money for a boy of nine in those days.

Another wonderful memory is of the great annual evening celebrations put on by the Hampshire Down Sheep Breeders Association, with a three-course meal and after-dinner speakers. It was held each year at the Red Lion in Salisbury, the main course being lamb, supplied by one of the local breeders.

I can't remember what year it was, about 1950 I think, when the Royal Show was held at Lincoln. After the judging was over, some of the shepherds, including Father, Wilf Pitt, Ted Frampton and one or two more, would go out of the showground and find the nearest pub. One night they had far too much to drink. As they came back into the ground, the first stand was nearly all wheelbarrows. They borrowed two of these, sat in them and pushed each other up to the sheep lines.

The next morning, when they were sober, they realised what they had done. It was me, 'the boy', who had to take the wheelbarrows back and apologise to the man on the stand. He just laughed. He knew it was just good-hearted fun. That's the way it was in those days. How things have changed!

I've looked back on my life and written most of these stories about it sitting in my little office, overlooking the Manor Farm and the lovely gardens of Oliver and Sue Simon, here at Stourton Caundle, and it really has kept me in touch with the land I yearn for so much. The gardens are an inspiration both to me and to the whole village, and are open to the public almost every year. The other people I owe a massive debt to are Ralph and Dianne Mowat. They've taken all these stories of mine and helped me join them up into the story of my life. And what a life it has been!

I believe that more people should pause for a moment and write down their memories, if only for family posterity. A lot of changes have taken place in the last hundred years. I'm not so sure about the next twenty years, let alone the next century.

This is our home now, at The Trooper, a truly unspoilt Dorset pub in the heart of the village, in the countryside I love so much. I've decided to end with the opening and closing lines from John F. Angus's poem, 'The Village Pub', which both captures my feelings about my own life and perfectly describes what The Trooper means to Sue and I:

'Its timbered frame has played its part
For all who care to see
A slight twist here, a bulge just there,

Some tiny cracks maybe.
Its walls were made of local stone,
In those days built to last,
If they could talk they would recall
The epics of our past

So as you sit in comfort, about to sup your ale,
Just glance up at those rafters,
Before you start your tale.
'Cos up there on those beams,
Chopped out of English Oak,
Our history lies recorded,
Etched in dust and smoke.'